TEACHER'S PET PUBLICATIONS

LITPLAN TEACHER PACK
for
The Joy Luck CLub
based on the book by
Amy Tan

Written by
Marion B. Hoffman & Mary B. Collins

© 1999 Teacher's Pet Publications
All Rights Reserved

This **LitPlan** for Amy Tan's
The Joy Luck Club
has been brought to you by Teacher's Pet Publications, Inc.

Copyright Teacher's Pet Publications 1999
11504 Hammock Point
Berlin MD 21811

Only the student materials in this unit plan
such as worksheets, study questions, assignment sheets, and tests
may be reproduced multiple times for use in the purchaser's classroom.

For any additional copyright questions,
contact Teacher's Pet Publications.

www.tpet.com

TABLE OF CONTENTS - *The Joy Luck Club*

Introduction	7
Unit Objectives	10
Reading Assignment Sheet	11
Unit Outline	12
Study Questions (Short Answer)	15
Quiz/Study Questions (Multiple Choice)	34
Pre-reading Vocabulary Worksheets	69
Lesson One (Introductory Lesson)	89
Nonfiction Assignment Sheet	91
Oral Reading Evaluation Form	92
Writing Assignment 1	94
Writing Assignment 2	97
Writing Assignment 3	105
Writing Evaluation Form	98
Vocabulary Review Activities	106
Extra Writing Assignments/Discussion ?s	108
Unit Review Activities	111
Unit Tests	115
Unit Resource Materials	141
Vocabulary Resource Materials	157

ABOUT THE AUTHOR

A great deal of information is available about Amy Tan's personal and professional lives. Perhaps this is because her writing is clearly so overlaid with biography and autobiography. It might also be because her stories have so touched the hearts of her readers. And it might be because her enormous literary popularity coincides with the tremendous growth of the internet as a means of instant communication. Information about her seems to have popped up daily on many different web sites.

A quick search of the internet, the local bookstore, or the neighborhood library should turn up much solid information about this most interesting Chinese American writer. What follows here is some basic information about the author and her work.

Amy Tan's first novel, **The Joy Luck Club**, originally to be titled **Wind and Water**, was published in 1989. Technically neither a novel nor a short story collection, **The Joy Luck Club** is instead a series of interrelated stories for and about mothers and their daughters. There are sixteen stories in all told in groups of four: six are told by mothers and the remaining ten are told by their daughters.

The order of the stories is interesting: The first group begins with one story told by a daughter followed by three told by mothers. All of the eight stories in the second and third groups are related by daughters. Then the fourth and final group reverses the order of the first group: the first three stories are told by mothers and the last story is told by a daughter.

Tan's language is very easy to understand. She speaks in a clear, direct voice that makes her story telling compelling. Although some of the stories seem fairly simplistic, some contain enough metaphor and allusion to require a second or possibly a third reading. And because all of them deal with deep, meaningful emotions and complicated psychological relationships, several are very moving.

The Joy Luck Club has been translated into many different languages. It was a finalist for the National Book Award and the National Book Critics Circle Award in 1989. It received the 1990 Bay Area Reviewers Award for Fiction. For months **The Joy Luck Club** was on **The New York Times** bestseller list, and the rights to the paperback edition were sold for over one million dollars. The book has also been made into a film for which Amy Tan helped to write the screen play.

Her second important work was **The Kitchen God's Wife**, published in 1991. Her most recent publication was **The Hundred Secret Senses** in 1996. She has also published two children's picture books, **The Moon Lady** and **The Chinese Siamese Cat**.

Amy Tan was born on February 19, 1952, in Oakland, California. She grew up in the San Francisco Bay area, moving frequently from one place to another as her father, a Baptist minister, accepted new ministries. After graduating from high school in Montreux, Switzerland, Tan attended a few different colleges. Ultimately she received a bachelor's degree from San Jose

State University in 1973 and was awarded a master's degree in linguistics from the same university in 1974.

For over twenty years, Tan has been married to Louis DeMattei. They have homes in the Presidio Heights section of San Francisco and in New York City.

Amy Tan's father was John Yueh-han, who worked for the U.S. Information Service prior to coming to the United States in the late 1940's. Educated as an electrical engineer and a minister, Tan's father was born in Wuhan, China.

Tan's mother, Daisy Ching (born Tu Ching) was married once before, in China, for twelve years, to a man who abused her. Daisy Ching had three other daughters and lost track of them after the Communists took over in China. Because it was then illegal for a woman to leave her husband, Daisy Ching spent some months in prison in China when her former marriage and circumstances were revealed.

Daisy Ching met John Yueh-han during the 1940's in China. He came to the United States ahead of his wife and worked diligently to have her join him in this country. Following her prison term, she immigrated to America in 1949.

The year 1967 was an incredibly difficult one for Amy Tan and her family. First her older brother, Peter, and then their father, was diagnosed with malignant brain tumors and died within six months of each other. That same year, Amy Tan's mother was also diagnosed with a brain tumor, but fortunately hers was benign.

Following the deaths of her husband and son, Daisy Ching saw fit to take her daughter and remaining son to Europe. While there, Amy and her brother attended school in Switzerland. Whereas Tan had always been the only non-Caucasian student in her schools in America, in Switzerland, she was one of a large group of children from other countries. She finished her high school studies in Europe.

Amy Tan's professional life is often said to have started when authorities closed her local library. At age eight Tan wrote an essay entitled, "What the Library Means to Me," which was published in **The Press Democrat** in Santa Rosa, California. The essay extolled the benefits of the public library system.

Although Tan worked at a variety of jobs, such as bartender, switchboard operator, pizza maker, and counselor for developmentally disabled children, her writing career really started when she began working as a business writer. At first she worked for different companies; then she became a free lance writer. Her biggest drawback as a free lance writer was that she took on so many projects that she often was working 60-80 hours a week just to keep ahead.

In 1985 she had a short story published in **Seventeen** magazine. The story was noticed by a book agent who asked her to write an outline for a book. That book was **The Joy Luck Club**, reportedly written by Tan in four months, and published by Putnam.

Amy Tan's mother and other female family members have been a great inspiration for Tan's writing. Through the years, though, Tan's rebelliousness and life choices often placed her at odds with her mother. Like many of the daughters in **The Joy Luck Club**, Amy Tan was a rebellious person who, in her youth, preferred not to be Chinese but to be entirely American.

It was not until she was thirty-five years old, visited China, and met her half-sisters there that Tan developed a real appreciation for her Chinese roots. During the intervening years, two of her half-sisters have relocated to the United States.

As Amy Tan matured, so did her relationship with her mother. Once when Daisy Ching was ill, she reportedly asked her daughter what she would remember of her mother. Amy Tan's dedication of **The Joy Luck Club** speaks simply but eloquently to that question:

> *To my mother*
> *and the memory of her mother*
>
> *You asked me once*
> *what I would remember.*
>
> *This, and much more.*

Note: Much information is available about Amy Tan. One book that might be especially useful and enjoyable in middle and high school classrooms is one of the People To Know books: **Amy Tan Author of The Joy Luck Club**
        by Barbara Kramer
        Enslow Publishers, Inc., Springfield, N.J., 07081

INTRODUCTION

This unit plan is designed to develop students' reading, writing, thinking, reasoning, and language skills as well as their imagination and sense of discovery. It meets these goals through a series of exercises, assignments, and activities related to **The Joy Luck Club** by Amy Tan. The plan includes twenty-five pre-planned daily lessons based on the book's sixteen stories as well as extra resource materials created to facilitate the teaching and learning of Tan's book.

The **introductory lesson** introduces students to some information about China to establish a framework for their reading about Chinese mothers and daughters over a span of years. Be sure to explain the lesson's purpose to students and encourage them to keep the new information in mind as they read **The Joy Luck Club**.

Because the **reading assignments** are based on the individual stories in **The Joy Luck Club**, they vary in length from *Scar* with nineteen pages to *Magpies* with thirty-three. The average reading assignment comes out to nearly twenty pages. Given the general complexity of the stories, we believe that they must be read and discussed individually.

The **study questions**-both short answer and multiple choice-are fact based. Students can find the answers to the 144 questions right in the text. We advise using the short answer version of the questions as study guides for students and using the multiple choice version for occasional or regular quizzes. Answer keys are available for all of the questions. If your school has the appropriate machinery, you might like to make transparencies of your answer keys for use with an overhead projector.

The **vocabulary work** is intended to enrich students' vocabularies as well as to aid in their understanding of the stories. Along with each reading assignment, have students complete a two-part worksheet on words from the upcoming section of the text they are reading. There are 119 separate words.

Part I focuses on students' use of their general knowledge and contextual clues by giving the sentence in which the word appears in the text. Students are to write down what they think the words mean based on usage. Part II nails down the definitions of the words by asking students to match the words to their correct dictionary definitions. By the time students have finished a reading assignment and concurrently done the vocabulary work, they should have a thorough understanding of each of the words.

After each reading assignment, students will go back and formulate answers to each of the short answer questions. Discussion of these questions serves as a **review** of the most important events and ideas presented in the reading assignments.

Joy Luck Club - Introduction - page 2

After students complete extra discussion questions, there is a **vocabulary review** lesson which pulls together all of the vocabulary lists for the reading assignments and gives students a review of all of the words studied.

In this unit plan, daily lessons twenty-one and twenty-two are devoted to **extra discussion questions/writing assignments**. These questions focus on interpretation, critical analysis, and personal response. They employ a variety of thinking skills and add to the students' understanding of **The Joy Luck Club**. These questions may be used as either individual or group activities, but group work will better aid the students. Using the information they have acquired so far through individual work and class discussions, students can get together to further examine the text and to brainstorm ideas relating to the book's ideas, themes, and characters.

There is also opportunity for students to gain experience in **oral presentations** in reading, in role playing, and in acting like one of the characters. An Oral Reading Evaluation form is provided for evaluating the reading.

There are three **writing assignments** in this unit plan. The first is to express personal opinions: students have an opportunity to think about and to present their personal views of some family relationships. This assignment helps students to think about the kind of intricate relationships presented in **The Joy Luck Club**. The second assignment is to inform: students are encouraged to think about a game they enjoy playing, like several of the characters play mahjong in the book. Students need to think through the game they choose and to inform others how to play it. The third assignment gives students a chance to write to persuade: writing from the standpoint of one of the "aunties" in the book, students try to persuade one of the daughters to take a different view of her own mother. The students learn to think about how to present one of the mothers favorably and have their attention drawn to Amy Tan's technique of presenting characters in a variety of different lights and from a variety of different points of view.

In addition, there is a **nonfiction assignment**. Students are required to read a piece of nonfiction related in some way to **The Joy Luck Club**. After reading their nonfiction pieces, students fill out a worksheet on which they answer questions regarding facts, interpretation, criticism, and personal opinion. Students are given a wide range of possible topics for the nonfiction assignment and should be encouraged to write on something of particular interest to them.

The **review lesson** pulls together all of the aspects of the unit. You are given a choice of activities or games to use. All serve the same basic function of reviewing all of the information presented in the unit.

Joy Luck Club - Introduction - page 3

The **unit tests** give you an opportunity to test students' acquired knowledge using short answer questions, multiple choice, vocabulary, and essay. For your convenience, two tests are available for short answer and two for multiple choice. An advanced test is also available should you choose to use it. Answers are provided for all questions on the short answer, multiple choice, and vocabulary tests. Approaches to answers are suggested even for the essay tests.

There are additional **support materials** included with this unit. The **extra activities packet** gives suggestions for an in-class library, crossword and word search puzzles related to the novel, and extra vocabulary worksheets. A list of **bulletin board ideas** gives you suggestions for bulletin boards to go along with this unit. In addition, there is a list of **extra class activities** which might enhance the unit or serve as a substitution for an exercise that you might feel is less appropriate for your class.

Answer keys are located directly after the **reproducible student materials** throughout the unit. The student materials may be reproduced for use in your classroom without infringement of copyrights. No other portion of this unit may be reproduced without the written consent of Teacher's Pet Publications, Inc.

UNIT OBJECTIVES - *The Joy Luck Club*

1. Through reading Tan's ***The Joy Luck Club***, students will gain a better understanding of some important ideas presented in the book, such as Chinese customs and superstitions, learn some difficulties and joys associated with mother/daughter relationships, see how the generation gap can sometimes make communication between people difficult, to understand the four mothers and four daughters better through a series of sixteen stories told from various points of view.

2. Students will demonstrate their understanding of the text on four levels: factual, interpretive, critical and personal.

3. Students will have the opportunity to express their personal opinions on the aforementioned themes.

4. Students will be given the opportunity to practice reading aloud and silently to improve their skills in each area.

5. Students will answer questions to demonstrate their knowledge and understanding of the main events and characters in ***The Joy Luck Club.***

6. Students will enrich their vocabularies and improve their understanding of the novel through the vocabulary lessons prepared for use in conjunction with the novel.

7. The writing assignments in this unit are geared to several purposes:
   a. To have students demonstrate their abilities to inform, to persuade, or to express their own personal ideas
      Note: Students will demonstrate ability to write effectively to <u>inform</u> by developing and organizing facts to convey information. Students will demonstrate the ability to write effectively to <u>persuade</u> by selecting and organizing relevant information, establishing an argumentative purpose, and by designing an appropriate strategy for an identified audience. Students will demonstrate the ability to write effectively to <u>express personal ideas</u> by selecting a form and its appropriate elements.
   b. To check the students' reading comprehension
   c. To make students think about the ideas presented by the novel
   d. To encourage logical thinking
   e. To provide an opportunity to practice good grammar and improve students' use of the English language.

8. Students will read aloud, report, and participate in large and small group discussions to improve their public speaking and personal interaction skills.

READING ASSIGNMENT SHEET - *The Joy Luck Club*

Date Assigned	RA #	Reading Assignment (Chapters)	Completion Date
	1	The Joy Luck Club Scar	
	2	The Red Candle	
	3	The Moon Lady	
	4	Rules of the Game The Voice from the Wall	
	5	Half and Half	
	6	Two Kinds	
	7	Rice Husband	
	8	Four Directions	
	9	Without Wood	
	10	Best Quality	
	11	Magpies	
	12	Waiting Between the Trees Double Face	
	13	A Pair of Tickets	

UNIT OUTLINE - *The Joy Luck Club*

1 Introduction	2 PVR RA#1 PVR RA#2	3 ?s RA 1&2 PVR RA#3	4 ?s RA 3 Writing Assignment #1 PVR RA#4	5 ? RA #4 PVR RA#5
6 ?s RA 5 PVR RA#6	7 ?s RA 6 Nonfiction Assignment	8 Writing Assignment #2 PVR RA#7	9 ?s RA 7 Role Play PVR RA#8	10 ?s RA 8 PVR RA#9
11 ?s RA 9 Chess	12 PVR RA#10	13 ?s RA 10 PVR RA#11	14 ?s RA 11 Nonfiction PVR RA#12	15 ?s RA #12 Character Study PVR RA#13
16 ?s RA13 Writing Assignment #3	17 Vocabulary Review	18 Discussion Preparation	19 Discussion	20 Unit Review
20 Unit Test				

Key: P = Preview Study Questions   V = Vocabulary Work   R = Read

STUDY GUIDE QUESTIONS

SHORT ANSWER STUDY QUESTIONS - *The Joy Luck Club*

SECTION 1 - FEATHERS FROM A THOUSAND LI AWAY

This series of stories addresses the desire of the Chinese mothers for their daughters to have better lives in America than they had in China. The better life is symbolized in the swan one mother brought with her. Immigration officials took it from her, leaving her with only one feather to remind her of what she had left behind. Even when her daughter's life fails to live up to her expectations, the mother keeps the one feather and thinks that one day she will use it to explain, in perfect English, all of her good intentions for her daughter.

The Joy Luck Club told by Jing-mei Woo
1. Why was Jing-mei taking part in the Joy Luck Club?
2. How many Joy Luck Clubs have there been?
3. Why did Jing-mei's mother form the Joy Luck Club in Kweilin?
4. Why did the women in the club call it Joy Luck?
5. What surprising information did Jing-mei finally learn from her mother's story about leaving Kweilin?
6. How do the people at the San Francisco Joy Luck Club eat?
7. Why did "the aunties" give Jing-mei $1200 in an envelope?
8. What do "the aunties" want Jing-mei to tell her sisters in China?
9. What surprising thing does Jing-mei tell her "aunties" about her own mother?
10. What does Jing-mei promise "the aunties" at the end of the story?

Scar told by An-Mei Hsu
1. What did An-mei's mother do to become a ghost?
2. What did it mean in An-mei's family to become a ghost?
3. Why did An-mei's grandmother say bad things about her own grandchildren?
4. What happened to the greedy girl in An-mei's grandmother's story?
5. In An-mei's grandmother's story, what happened to the little girl who refused to listen to her elders?
6. Why was An-mei told never to say her mother's name?
7. In *Scar*, what is the definition of **shou**?
8. What is An-mei's "know-nothing face"?
9. What does An-mei remember about her mother from when An-mei was four?
10. After An-mei was burned, what did her grandmother tell her that made her get better fast?
11. What does An-mei's mother do to show her love and respect for her own mother?
12. In the story, what does An-mei learn from her own mother?

The Red Candle told by Lindo Jong
1. How did Lindo Jong become engaged to her future husband, Tyan-yu?
2. How did Lindo first become a member of the Huang household?
3. What gift did Lindo's mother give to Lindo as the family moved away?
4. How did Tyan-yu make Lindo cry the first night she lived in his house?
5. What did Lindo's mother-in-law instruct the servants to teach Lindo?
6. What promise did Lindo make to herself on her wedding day?

Joy Luck Club - Short Answer Study Questions - page 2

7. Why was Lindo unafraid while she was led down a path on her wedding day?
8. What was the red candle's significance and what was supposed to happen to it?
9. What lie did the matchmaker's servant tell?
10. What mark on Tyan-yu did Lindo use to "prove" her marriage was rotting?
11. How did Lindo escape from the marriage to Tyan-yu?
12. What is the significance in the story of the Festival of Pure Brightness?

The Moon Lady told by Ying-ying St. Clair
1. What does Ying-yin say her earliest recollection is?
2. Why does the Amah tell Ying-ying that she must keep her wishes secret?
3. How did Ying-ying wind up in the water?
4. What is the ultimate fate of the Moon Lady?
5. What was the effect on Ying-ying of listening to the Moon Lady's story?
6. What does the Moon Lady represent for Ying-ying?
7. What wish did Ying-ying ask for from the Moon Lady?
8. How does Ying-ying's story reflect her life and that of her daughter?

SECTION 2 - THE TWENTY-SIX MALIGNANT GATES

These stories address the mothers telling their daughters how to live. The daughters reject their mothers' ideas, but what the mothers say comes true. This point is symbolized in the mother who tells the daughter not to ride her bicycle around the corner because she will fall down and cry and not be heard by her mother. The daughter rejects the mother's ideas but then she jumps on her bicycle and falls even before she reaches the corner.

Rules of the Game told by Waverly Jong
1. What was "the art of invisible strength" that Waverly's mother taught her?
2. How did Waverly's mother demonstrate the art of invisible strength?
3. How did Waverly learn to play expert chess?
4. What would Waverly's mother say when she attended Waverly's chess exhibition games outdoors?
5. Why did Waverly run away?
6. How did Waverly's mother treat her when she returned home after running away?
7. What was Waverly's mother's view of "rules"?
8. At the end of the story, who is Waverly's imaginary chess opponent?

The Voice from the Wall told by Lena St. Clair
1. What does the dead beggar say when he returns?
2. How did the American immigration authorities categorize Lena's mother?
3. Why does Lena want to know "the worst possible thing that can happen" to her?
4. Why did Lena start telling lies?
5. What was Lena's great hope when the family moved out of Oakland?
6. What did Lena hear through the wall of the new apartment?

Joy Luck Club - Short Answer Study Questions - page 3

7. Why did the girl from next door leave her own apartment?
8. How did the girl from next door get out of Lena's bedroom?
9. What happened later that night after the girl and her mother had argued?
10. What hope did Lena have after watching the girl next door with her mother?

Half and Half told by Rose Hsu Jordan
1. What did Rose's mother used to carry to church services at the First Chinese Baptist Church?
2. What makes Rose sure that her mother knows the Bible is still under a table leg in her kitchen?
3. How did the decision making start and then change in Rose's marriage?
4. What did Rose find out "faith" was?
5. What was the name of Rose's mother's little Chinese book and what was in it?
6. What did Rose and her mother do early on the morning after Rose's brother drowned?
7. Why did Rose's mother throw her blue sapphire ring into the water?
8. Why did Rose's mother throw an inner tube attached to a fishing pole into the water?
9. When Rose took the Bible out from under the table leg, what did she find written in it?
10. Why was Bing's name written in pencil?

Two Kinds told by Jing-mei Woo
1. What made Jing-mei's mother think that Jing-mei could be a prodigy?
2. What did Jing-mei's mother lose in China?
3. How did Jing-mei first envision herself as a prodigy?
4. What would perfection have meant for Jing-mei while she was waiting to become a prodigy?
5. Why did Jing-mei's mother read so many magazines?
6. What happened to all of Jing-mei's mother's early efforts to find out what kind of prodigy Jing-mei should be?
7. What was wrong with Jing-mei's piano teacher and how did his defect affect her playing?
8. What piece did Jing-mei select for the talent show in the church hall?
9. Who was the only person in the church hall who thought Jing-mei's performance was good?
10. What did Jing-mei realize after she had played both "Pleading Child" and "Perfectly Contented" a few times?

Joy Luck Club - Short Answer Study Questions - page 4

AMERICAN TRANSLATION

The stories in this section continue the clash between the values of the Chinese mothers and the new lives embraced by the American daughters. This is symbolized in the mirrored armoire in the master suite of the daughter's new condominium. It's mirrors are at the foot of the bed and will reflect happiness away from the daughter. The mother placed a gilt-edged mirror on the headboard of the bed to bring the daughter "peach-blossom luck," fertility, the grandchildren that the grandmother-to-be desires.

Rice Husband told by Lena St. Clair
1. What does the saying, "If the lips are gone, the teeth will be cold," mean?
2. What does Lena's mother see?
3. What are the three things that Lena's mother predicted that came true?
4. What does Lena think her mother will see during her visit with her and Harold?
5. What physical aspect of Lena's house does her mother connect with a feeling?
6. What food does Harold not realize that Lena doesn't eat?
7. Why does Harold hate it when Lena cries?
8. When Lena says, "I knew it would happen," what question does her mother ask?
9. Why does the marble end table collapse?

Four Directions told by Waverly Jong
1. What did Waverly want to tell her mother at lunch?
2. What did Waverly's mother do when she found that Waverly had eloped with her first husband?
3. Why did Waverly first stop playing chess as a child?
4. What special thing could Waverly's mother do to change Waverly's view of a person?
5. What mistake did Rich make about the wine at the dinner with Waverly's family?
6. Why was Waverly so anxious that her mother was the queen while she, Waverly, was the pawn?
7. In what way was Waverly confused about where her mother came from?
8. What trip is Waverly contemplating at the end of the story and with whom would she travel?

Without Wood told by Rose Hsu Jordan
1. When Rose was little, what did she believe?
2. Why did Rose's mother say that Rose was "without wood"?
3. Why did Rose stay in bed for three days?
4. Where did Rose tell Ted she was going to live?
5. When Rose says that Ted is **hulihudu**, what does she mean?
6. What does Rose's mother plan in Rose's garden?

Best Quality by Jing-mei Woo
1. What is Jing-mei's "life's importance" gift from her mother?
2. Why did Jing-mei's mother not want to keep the crab that had lost a leg?
3. Why did Jing-mei leave the room while the crabs were being steamed?
4. How do Jing-mei and her mother disagree in regard to Waverly Jong?
5. How did Waverly insult Jing-mei professionally?
6. Who got the crab with the missing leg?

QUEEN MOTHER OF THE WESTERN SKIES

This series of stories represent the Chinese mothers trying to pass along the message that the daughters should lose their innocence but not their hope. This is symbolized by the woman teasing her baby granddaughter and remembering how she went from freedom and innocence and laughter to learning to protect herself. She taught her daughter to protect herself by shedding her own innocence. Now, seeing the laughing baby, the grandmother wonders if her daughter can learn through the child to keep her hope and to laugh forever.

Magpies told by An-mei Hsu
1. In what way does An-mei say that all people born girls are alike?
2. What did it mean to An-mei to be raised "the Chinese way"?
3. How did An-mei's mother dishonor her widowhood?
4. What did the turtle in the pond do to An-mei's tears?
5. What happened to the eggs that poured out of the turtle's beak?
6. What emotion described the magpies?
7. What did the story of the turtles and the magpies teach An-mei's mother to do?
8. How did An-mei learn not to listen to something meaningless calling to her?
9. Why did An-mei's mother send An-mei out of their bedroom at night?
10. Why did An-mei's mother become Wu Tsing's concubine?
11. How did An-mei's mother die?
12. What promise did Wu Tsing make to An-mei's mother after she died?
13. What does An-mei say that her daughter's psychiatrist is?
14. How did the tired Chinese peasants get rid of the birds that were drinking their tears and eating their seeds?

Waiting Between the Trees told by Ying-ying St. Clair
1. How has Lena St. Clair unknowingly insulted her mother by giving her the guest bedroom in her home?
2. What did Lena do when she was born?
3. When Ying-ying was a young girl in Wushi, she was **lihai**. What does that mean?
4. When did Ying-ying begin to know things before they happened?
5. What sign happened to convince Ying-ying that she would marry the man who was a guest at her house?
6. Why did Ying-ying's husband leave her?

Joy Luck Club - Short Answer Study Questions - page 6

7. What is the difference between what Lena sees in her mother and what her mother really is?
8. Why, according to Ying-ying, is the tiger gold and black?
9. Why does Ying-ying abort her first child?
10. What did Ying-ying do for ten years at the country home of her cousin's family?
11. What did Ying-ying give up when she married St. Clair?
12. At the end of the story, what does Ying-ying want to do for her daughter?

Double Face told by Lindo Jong
1. Why does Waverly Jong want to go to China?
2. Why does Waverly especially want to be Chinese?
3. Why could Lindo's children not have American circumstances and Chinese character?
4. Who first taught Lindo about America?
5. What kind of job did Lindo get in the cookie factory?
6. What was the fortune inside the cookie that Lindo gave to Tin?
7. Why does Waverly like the fact that she and her mother have crooked noses?
8. At the end of the story, what is Lindo wondering about?

A Pair of Tickets told by Jing-mei Woo
1. Why does Jing-mei feel different as her train leaves the Hong Kong border and enters Shenzhen, China?
2. Where is Jing-mei meeting her two half-sisters?
3. How did the half-sisters learn that their mother was dead?
4. How did Jing-mei learn the details of what happened to her half-sisters?
5. Why did Jing-mei's mother actually leave the babies?
6. Who found the babies?
7. What are the two different Chinese meanings of Suyuan, Jing-mei's mother's name?
8. What are the meanings of Jing-mei's name?

KEY: SHORT ANSWER STUDY QUESTIONS

SECTION 1 - FEATHERS FROM A THOUSAND LI AWAY

The Joy Luck Club told by Jing-mei Woo

1. Why was Jing-mei taking part in the Joy Luck Club?
   Because her mother had died and she was asked by her father to be "the fourth corner" at the game

2. How many Joy Luck Clubs have there been?
   There have been two Joy Luck Clubs.

3. Why did Jing-mei's mother form the Joy Luck Club in Kweilin?
   She formed the club in Kweilin to give herself and some friends a diversion from the horrors of war.

4. Why did the women in the club call it Joy Luck?
   Because the women hoped to be lucky, and that hope was their only joy

5. What surprising information did Jing-mei finally learn from her mother's story about leaving Kweilin?
   She finally realized that her mother had left her two daughters behind.

6. How do the people at the San Francisco Joy Luck Club eat?
   They eat as though they had been starving.

7. Why did "the aunties" give Jing-mei $1200 in an envelope?
   They collected the money so that Jing-mei could go to China and meet her half-sisters.

8. What do "the aunties" want Jing-mei to tell her sisters in China?
   They want her to tell her half-sisters about her mother.

9. What surprising thing does Jing-mei tell her "aunties" about her own mother?
   Jing-mei tells her "aunties" that she really doesn't know anything about her mother.

10. What does Jing-mei promise "the aunties" at the end of the story?
    She promises that she will tell her sisters everything about her mother.

Scar told by An-Mei Hsu

1. What did An-mei's mother do to become a ghost?
   An-mei's mother became a ghost by showing disrespect for her family.

2. What did it mean in An-mei's family to become a ghost?
   That everyone was forbidden to talk about the person

3. Why did An-mei's grandmother say bad things about her own grandchildren?
   She said bad things so that ghosts would think the children were not worth stealing.

4. What happened to the greedy girl in An-mei's grandmother's story?
   She grew fatter and fatter and finally poisoned herself after refusing to say whose child she carried.

5. In An-mei's grandmother's story, what happened to the little girl who refused to listen to her elders?
   She refused her aunt's request and a little ball fell from her ear and all her brains poured out.

6. Why was An-mei told never to say her mother's name?
   Because to say her mother's name was to spit on her father's grave

7. In *Scar*, what is the definition of **shou**?
   Shou is having no respect for ancestors or family.

8. What is An-mei's "know-nothing face"?
   It is the face she puts on when she doesn't want to reveal her true emotions.

9. What does An-mei remember about her mother from when An-mei was four?
   She remembers that her mother returned to the family and was chased away the same night after An-mei was burned by the hot soup.

10. After An-mei was burned, what did her grandmother tell her that made her get better fast?
    Her grandmother told her that her mother had left and would forget An-mei if An-mei didn't get better fast.

11. What does An-mei's mother do to show her love and respect for her own mother?
    She returns to her family and cuts off a piece of her own flesh, puts it in a soup, and serves it to her dying mother.

12. In the story, what does An-mei learn from her own mother?
    She learns that one's love and respect for one's mother is deep within one's bones.

The Red Candle told by Lindo Jong

1. How did Lindo Jong become engaged to her future husband, Tyan-yu?
   A match was arranged through a matchmaker when Lindo was two and Tyan-yu was only one.

2. How did Lindo first become a member of the Huang household?
   When she was twelve, her family moved away and sent her to live with the Huang family.

3. What gift did Lindo's mother give to Lindo as the family moved away?
   She gave Lindo her **chang**, a necklace made out of a tablet of red jade.

4. How specifically did Tyan-yu make Lindo cry the first night she lived in his house?
   By complaining that the soup was not hot enough, spilling the bowl as if it were an accident, waiting until she sat down before demanding more rice, and asking why she had such an unpleasant face when looking at him

5. What did Lindo's mother-in-law instruct the servants to teach Lindo?
   She instructed them to teach her to perform a variety of household duties so that she would be a good, obedient wife.

6. What promise did Lindo make to herself on her wedding day?
   She promised herself that she would always remember her parents' wishes but would never forget herself.

7. Why was Lindo unafraid while she was led down a path on her wedding day?
   Because she could see what was inside herself

8. What was the red candle's significance and what was supposed to happen to it?
   The red candle symbolized Lindo's marriage to Tyan-yu, and it was supposed to be lit at both ends and kept burning all night long.

9. What lie did the matchmaker's servant tell?
   She said that the red candle had burned at both ends all night long.

10. What mark on Tyan-yu did Lindo use to "prove" her marriage was rotting?
    She used a small black mole on his back.

11. How did Lindo escape from the marriage to Tyan-yu?
    She convinced them that the pregnant servant girl was really of imperial blood and was Tyan-yu's spiritual wife.

12. Specifically what is the significance in the story of the Festival of Pure Brightness?
It is the day on which Lindo carried out her plan and a day she still celebrates by taking off all her bracelets and remembering the day when she finally knew a genuine thought and could follow where it went.

The Moon Lady told by Ying-ying St. Clair

1. What does Ying-yin say her earliest recollection is?
Her earliest recollection is telling the Moon Lady her secret wish.

2. Why does the amah tell Ying-ying that she must keep her wishes secret?
Because if she tells her secret wishes, it will no longer be a wish but will become a selfish desire

3. How did Ying-ying wind up in the water?
She fell off the back of the boat.

4. What is the ultimate fate of the Moon Lady?
To live on the moon while her husband lives on the sun; to forever seek her own selfish wishes

5. What was the effect on Ying-ying of listening to the Moon Lady's story?
The story made Ying-ying cry and shake with despair.

6. What does the Moon Lady represent for Ying-ying?
The Moon Lady represented an illusion, a wish granted that could not be trusted.

7. What wish did Ying-ying ask for from the Moon Lady?
She asked to be found.

8. How does Ying-ying's story reflect her life and that of her daughter?
She says that she and her daughter are both lost.

SECTION 2 - THE TWENTY-SIX MALIGNANT GATES

Rules of the Game told by Waverly Jong

1. What was "the art of invisible strength" that Waverly's mother taught her?
It was a strategy for winning arguments and gaining respect from others.

2. How did Waverly's mother demonstrate the art of invisible strength to Waverly?
She gave Waverly a gift of salted plums precisely because she kept quiet and didn't request them.

3. How did Waverly learn to play expert chess?
   In the beginning she taught herself and then she played with Lau Po.

4. What would Waverly's mother say when she attended Waverly's chess exhibition games outdoors?
   Waverly's mother would say, "Is luck."

5. Why did Waverly run away?
   Because her mother was embarrassing her and showing off

6. How did Waverly's mother treat her when she returned home after running away?
   Her mother treated her as though she didn't exist.

7. What was Waverly's mother's view of "rules"?
   She believed that people from foreign countries must learn the American "rules."

8. At the end of the story, who is Waverly's imaginary chess opponent?
   Her mother is her imaginary chess opponent.

The Voice from the Wall told by Lena St. Clair

1. What is the final thing the dead beggar says when he returns?
   He says that the worst is on the other side.

2. How did the American immigration authorities categorize Lena's mother?
   They categorized her as a "displaced person."

3. Why does Lena want to know "the worst possible thing that can happen" to her?
   She felt that if she knew the worst possible thing, then she could avoid it.

4. Why did Lena start telling lies?
   She started telling lies to prevent bad things from happening in the future.

5. What was Lena's great hope when the family moved out of Oakland?
   That she might be able to leave all the old fears behind

6. What did Lena hear through the wall of the new apartment?
   She heard the mother and daughter next door arguing violently.

7. Why did the girl from next door leave her own apartment?
   She left because her mother kicked her out of her apartment.

8. How did the girl from next door get out of Lena's bedroom?
   She climbed out onto the fire escape and back into her own apartment.

9. What happened later that night after the girl and her mother had argued?
The girl and her mother cried and laughed and shouted with love.

10. What hope did Lena have after watching the girl next door with her mother?
That things could be better than they appeared.

Half and Half told by Rose Hsu Jordan

1. What did Rose's mother used to carry to church services at the First Chinese Baptist Church?
A small leatherette Bible

2. What makes Rose sure that her mother knows the Bible is still under a table leg in her kitchen?
Because her mother is not the greatest housekeeper and yet the Bible is still clean white after twenty years

3. How did the decision making start and then change in Rose's marriage?
In the beginning, her husband made all of the decisions but then he lost a malpractice lawsuit and wanted her to make all of the decisions for them.

4. What did Rose find out "faith" was?
Rose found that "faith" was an illusion that somehow one is in control.

5. What was the name of Rose's mother's little Chinese book and what was in it?
The Twenty-six Malignant Gates showed how children are predisposed to certain dangers on certain days based on their Chinese birthdates.

6. What did Rose and her mother do early on the morning after Rose's brother drowned?
They went back to the beach to try to find him.

7. Why did Rose's mother throw her blue sapphire ring into the water?
She thought that it would divert the Coiling Dragon so that he would release her son from the water.

8. Why did Rose's mother throw an inner tube attached to a fishing pole into the water?
She believed that it would locate her lost son.

9. When her mother gave up finding Bing, what emotion did Rose feel?
She felt blinding anger.

10. When Rose took the Bible out from under the table leg, what did she find written in it?
She found her brother's name written in it in erasable pencil under "Deaths."

Two Kinds told by Jing-mei Woo

1. What made Jing-mei's mother think that Jing-mei could be a prodigy?
   She thought anyone could be anything they wanted to be in America.

2. What did Jing-mei's mother lose in China?
   She lost her mother and father, her family home, her first husband, and her twin baby daughters.

3. How did Jing-mei first envision herself as a prodigy?
   She envisioned herself as a dainty ballerina, the Christ child, or Cinderella.

4. What would perfection have meant for Jing-mei while she was waiting to become a prodigy?
   That her parents would adore her, she would be beyond reproach, and she would never feel the need to sulk for anything

5. Why did Jing-mei's mother read so many magazines?
   To find stories of remarkable children

6. What happened to all of Jing-mei's mother's early efforts to find out what kind of prodigy Jing-mei should be?
   They failed totally.

7. What was wrong with Jing-mei's piano teacher and how did his defect affect her playing?
   He was deaf and therefore could not tell whether Jing-mei was playing well or not.

8. What piece did Jing-mei select for the talent show in the church hall?
   The piece was called "Pleading Child."

9. Who was the only person in the church hall who thought Jing-mei's performance was good?
   The only person was her deaf piano teacher.

10. What did Jing-mei realize after she had played both "Pleading Child" and "Perfectly Contented" a few times?
    She realized that the two pieces were two halves of the same song.

AMERICAN TRANSLATION

Rice Husband told by Lena St. Clair

1. What does the saying, "If the lips are gone, the teeth will be cold," mean?
   That one thing is always the result of another

2. What does Lena's mother see?
   Lena's mother sees the bad things that will affect her family.

3. What are the three things that Lena's mother predicted that came true?
   A miscarriage, a bank failure, and Lena's father's death

4. What does Lena think her mother will see during her visit with her and Harold?
   Whatever is wrong

5. What physical aspect of Lena's house does her mother connect with a feeling?
   She says the slant of the floor makes her feel as if she is "running down."

6. What food does Harold not realize that Lena doesn't eat?
   Ice cream

7. Why does Harold hate it when Lena cries?
   He thinks it's manipulative.

8. Why does the marble end table collapse?
   It collapses because it is not sturdy.

9, When Lena says, "I knew it would happen," what questions does her mother ask?
   "Then why you don't stop it?"

Four Directions told by Waverly Jong

1. What did Waverly want to tell her mother at lunch?
   She wanted to tell her mother that she was getting married again.

2. What did Waverly's mother do when she found that Waverly had eloped with her first husband?
   She threw her shoe at them.

3. Why did Waverly first stop playing chess as a child?
   She first stopped because she felt her mother was trying to take all the credit for her winning.

4. What special thing could Waverly's mother do to change Waverly's view of a person?
   She could make Waverly see each of the person's traits in a new, negative way.

5. What mistake did Rich make about the wine at the dinner with Waverly's family?
   He drank two full glasses while everybody else had a half-inch "just for taste."

6. Why was Waverly so anxious that her mother was the queen while she, Waverly, was the pawn?
Because then Waverly could only run away while her mother could move in all directions

7. In what way was Waverly confused about where her mother came from?
She thought her mother was born in **Taiwan**, but her mother was really born in **Taiyuan**.

8. What trip is Waverly contemplating at the end of the story and with whom would she travel?
She is contemplating a trip to China made by herself, her mother, and Rich.

Without Wood told by Rose Hsu Jordan

1. When Rose was little, what did she believe her about her mother and mirrors?
She believed a mirror could see only her face but that her mother could see her inside out even when Rose was not in the room.

2. Why did Rose's mother say that Rose was "without wood"?
She explained that Rose was confused all of the time because she listened to too many people.

3. Why did Rose stay in bed for three days?
She stayed in bed for three days because her husband had left her and she was unable to make the simplest decisions.

4. Where did Rose tell Ted she was going to live?
She said she was going to continue to live in the house they had shared while they were married.

5. When Rose says that Ted is **hulihudu**, what does she mean?
She means that he is confused.

6. What does Rose's mother plant in Rose's garden?
Rose's mother plants weeds in her garden.

Best Quality by Jing-mei Woo

1. What is Jing-mei's "life's importance" gift from her mother?
It is a jade pendant on a gold chain.

2. Why did Jing-mei's mother not want to keep the crab that had lost a leg?
Because a missing leg on a crab is a bad sign on a Chinese New Year

3. Why did Jing-mei leave the room while the crabs were being steamed?
She left the room because she could not bear to remain while the crabs died.

4. How do Jing-mei and her mother disagree in regard to Waverly Jong?
   Jing-mei admires her while her mother says that Waverly is like a crab, always walking sideways, moving crooked.

5. How did Waverly insult Jing-mei professionally?
   She said that her firm had decided that Jing-mei's freelance work was unacceptable.

6. Who got the crab with the missing leg?
   Jing-mei's mother did.

QUEEN MOTHER OF THE WESTERN SKIES

Magpies told by An-mei Hsu

1. In what way does An-mei say that all people born girls are alike?
   They are all like stairs, one step after another, going up and down, but all going the same way.

2. What did it mean to An-mei to be raised "the Chinese way"?
   It meant being taught to desire nothing, to swallow other people's misery, and to eat one's own bitterness.

3. How did An-mei's mother dishonor her widowhood?
   She became the third concubine to a rich man.

4. What did the turtle in the pond do to An-mei's tears?
   The turtle ate An-mei's mother's tears.

5. What happened to the eggs that poured out of the turtle's beak?
   They became birds.

6. What emotion is usually associated with the magpies?
   The emotion is joy.

7. What did the turtle tell An-mei's mother as he drifted back into the pond?
   He told An-mei's mother that it is useless to cry.

8. How did An-mei learn not to listen to something meaningless calling to her?
   She learned this by learning to ignore the loud sound of the clock on her bedroom wall.

9. Why did An-mei's mother send An-mei out of their bedroom at night?
   Because Wu Tsing had arrived and wanted to be with her

10. Why did An-mei's mother become Wu Tsing's concubine?
    He raped her, thus giving her no choice but to stay with him as his concubine.

11. How did An-mei's mother die?
    She poisoned herself.

12. What promise did Wu Tsing make to An-mei's mother after she died?
    That he would raise her son and daughter as his honored children

13. What does An-mei say that her daughter's psychiatrist is?
    Just another bird drinking from Rose's misery

14. How did the tired Chinese peasants get rid of the birds that were drinking their tears and eating their seeds?
    They clapped their hands, banged sticks on pots and pans, and shouted at the birds to die.

Waiting Between the Trees told by Ying-ying St. Clair

1. How has Lena St. Clair unknowingly insulted her mother by giving her the guest bedroom in her home?
   Because the guest bedroom in Chinese custom should be the biggest and best bedroom and Lena's guest bedroom is tiny

2. What did Lena do when she was born?
   She sprang from her mother like a slippery fish.

3. When Ying-ying was a young girl in Wushi, she was **lihai**. What does that mean?
   It means that she was wild and stubborn.

4. When did Ying-ying begin to know things before they happened?
   She began to know these things the night her aunt got married when Ying-ying was sixteen.

5. What sign happened to convince Ying-ying that she would marry the man who was a guest at her house?
   A large wind blew in from the north and the flower on the table nearby split from its stem and fell at her feet

6. Why did Ying-ying's husband leave her?
   He left her to live with an opera singer.

7. What is the difference between what Lena sees in her mother and what her mother really is?
   Lena sees a small old lady but Ying-ying really is a tiger lady.

8. Why, according to Ying-ying, is the tiger gold and black?
   Because the gold side leaps with its fierce heart while the black side stands still with cunning and patience

9. Why does Ying-ying abort her first child?
   She aborts the child because she hates her husband, the child's father.

10. What did Ying-ying do for ten years at the country home of her cousin's family?
    She waited between the trees.

11. What did Ying-ying give up when she married St. Clair?
    She gave up her spirit.

12. At the end of the story, what does Ying-ying want to do for her daughter?
    She wants to give her daughter her own spirit.

Double Face told by Lindo Jong

1. Why does Waverly Jong want to go to China?
   She wants to go to China for her second honeymoon.

2. Why does Waverly especially want to be Chinese?
   Because it is so fashionable

3. Why could Lindo's children not have American circumstances and Chinese character?
   Because the two things do not mix

4. Who first taught Lindo about America?
   An American-raised Chinese girl in Peking

5. What kind of job did Lindo get in the cookie factory?
   She got a job forming Chinese fortune cookies out of hot dough.

6. What was the fortune inside the cookie that Lindo gave to Tin?
   The fortune was, "A house is not home when a spouse is not at home."

7. Why does Waverly like the fact that she and her mother have crooked noses?
   She likes their crooked noses because she thinks they make her and her mother look devious or two-faced.

8. At the end of the story, what is Lindo wondering about?
   She is wondering what she has lost in coming to America and what she has gotten back in return.

A Pair of Tickets told by Jing-mei Woo

1. Why does Jing-mei feel different as her train leaves the Hong Kong border and enters Shenzhen, China?
   Because she is becoming Chinese

2. Where is Jing-mei meeting her two half-sisters?
   She is meeting them in Shanghai.

3. How did the half-sisters learn that their mother was dead?
   They learned that their mother was dead when Auntie Lindo wrote a letter to them as Jing-mei asked her to do.

4. How did Jing-mei learn the details of what happened to her half-sisters?
   She learned the details from her father.

5. Why did Jing-mei's mother actually leave the babies?
   She left the babies because she thought she was going to die and didn't want them to die with her.

6. Who found the babies?
   The babies were found by an old peasant woman.

7. What are the two different Chinese meanings of Suyuan, Jing-mei's mother's name?
   "Long Cherished Wish" and "Long-Held Grudge."

8. What are the meanings of Jing-mei's name?
   "Just pure essence" and "younger sister."

MULTIPLE CHOICE QUIZZES - *Joy Luck Club*

SECTION 1 - FEATHERS FROM A THOUSAND LI AWAY

This series of stories addresses the desire of the Chinese mothers for their daughters to have better lives in America than they had in China. The better life is symbolized in the swan one mother brought with her. Immigration officials took it from her, leaving her with only one feather to remind her of what she had left behind. Even when her daughter's life fails to live up to her expectations, the mother keeps the one feather and thinks that one day she will use it to explain, in perfect English, all of her good intentions for her daughter.

The Joy Luck Club told by Jing-mei Woo

1. Why was Jing-mei taking part in the Joy Luck Club
    a. because she loved to play games with Chinese people
    b. because her mother had died and she was asked by her father to be "the fourth corner" at the game
    c. because there were very high prizes for winning at the club
    d. because she promised her mother to attend at least one meeting of the club

2. How many Joy Luck Clubs have there been?
    a. Sixteen
    b. Twelve
    c. One
    d. Two

3. Why did Jing-mei's mother form the Joy Luck Club in Kweilin?
    a. to be the first in her neighborhood to form a club
    b. because she loved to eat
    c. because she and her friends had nothing else to do
    d. to give herself and some friends a diversion from the horrors of war

4. Why did the women in the club call it Joy Luck?
    a. because the women hoped to be lucky, and that hope was their only joy
    b. because all of the good names for clubs were already taken
    c. because they wanted to use some of their own initials in the club name
    d. because "Joy Luck" in Chinese means "happy ladies"

5. What surprising information did Jing-mei finally learn from her mother's story about leaving Kweilin?
    a. She realized that her mother had been a shop girl in Kweilin.
    b. She realized that her mother's family had been royalty.
    c. She realized that her mother had left her two daughters behind.
    d. She realized that her mother was an inveterate liar.

Joy Luck Club - Multiple Choice Quizzes - page 2

6. How do the people at the San Francisco Joy Luck Club eat?
    a. very daintily
    b. as though they had been starving
    c. with many different utensils
    d. with much belching

7. Why did "the aunties" give Jing-mei $1200 in an envelope?
    a. They collected the money so that Jing-mei could go to China and meet her half-sisters.
    b. They won the money in a state lottery and wanted Jing-mei to have it.
    c. They had borrowed the money from Jing-mei and were paying it back.
    d. They had owed the money to Jing-mei's mother.

8. What do "the aunties" want Jing-mei to tell her sisters in China?
    a. the secrets of the Woo family
    b. about her mother
    c. about America
    d. about how their mother didn't want them

9. What surprising thing does Jing-mei tell her "aunties" about her own mother?
    a. She tells them that she didn't really love her mother.
    b. She tells them that her mother was much older than they had thought.
    c. She tells them that she really doesn't know anything about her mother.
    d. She tells them that her mother was living under an assumed name.

10. What does Jing-mei promise "the aunties" at the end of the story?
    a. that she won't waste their money
    b. that she will tell her sisters everything about her mother
    c. that she will never tell her sisters that their mother is dead
    d. that she will take good care of her father

Joy Luck Club - Multiple Choice Quizzes - page 3

Scar told by An-Mei Hsu

1. What did An-mei's mother do to become a ghost?
    a. She died.
    b. She became a Chinese gambler.
    c. She showed disrespect for her family.
    d. She forgot how to speak the Chinese language.

2. What did it mean in An-mei's family to become a ghost?
    a. It meant that everyone was forbidden to talk about the person.
    b. It meant that the person could never return home.
    c. It meant that the person was shunned by all other females.
    d. It meant that a funeral was held for the person.

3. Why did An-mei's grandmother say bad things about her own grandchildren?
    a. because she disliked their manners
    b. so that the ghosts would think the children were not worth stealing
    c. to make them mind her
    d. to frighten them into listening to her

4. What happened to the greedy girl in An-mei's grandmother's story?
    a. She was kidnapped by bank robbers.
    b. She grew fatter and fatter and finally poisoned herself after refusing to say whose child she carried.
    c. She kept wanting more and more things until finally there was nothing left for her to desire.
    d. She died and was buried on the same day.

5. In An-mei's grandmother's story, what happened to the little girl who refused to listen to her elders?
    a. She refused her aunt's request and a little ball fell from her ear and all her brains poured out.
    b. She was made to stay in her room for three whole days as punishment.
    c. She was whipped.
    d. She suddenly became unable to hear at all.

6. Why was An-mei told never to say her mother's name?
    a. because it was too hard for a child to pronounce
    b. because to say her mother's name was to spit on her father's grave
    c. because the soldiers would come to get her mother if they heard her name spoken out loud
    d. because to say her mother's name would mean her mother could return to the family

36

Joy Luck Club - Multiple Choice Quizzes - page 4

7. In *Scar*, what is the definition of **shou**?
   a. It means one will experience great happiness.
   b. It means one can never come back home.
   c. It means one will shed many tears.
   d. It means one has no respect for ancestors or family.

8. What is An-mei's "know-nothing face"?
   a. It is the face she wears in school to avoid being called on by the teacher.
   b. It is the face she wears when she has done something wrong.
   c. It is the face she puts on when she doesn't want to reveal her true emotions.
   d. It is the face she puts on when she is acting silly.

9. What does An-mei remember about her mother from when An-mei was four?
   a. She remembers that her mother got caught gambling.
   b. She remembers that her mother returned to the family and was chased away the same night after An-mei was burned by the hot soup.
   c. She remembers that her mother appeared to her in a dream on her birthday.
   d. She remembers that her mother and her uncle quarreled about money.

10. After An-mei was burned, what did her grandmother tell her that made her get better fast?
    a. Her grandmother told her that her mother had left and would forget An-mei if An-mei didn't get better fast.
    b. Her grandmother told her that she was behaving very badly.
    c. Her grandmother told her that the ghosts would get her if she didn't get better fast.
    d. Her grandmother told her that she would die.

11. What does An-mei's mother do to show her love and respect for her own mother?
    a. She bows deeply and calls her by a special name.
    b. She gets up early in the morning and fixes her a special meal.
    c. She returns to her family and cuts off a piece of her own flesh, puts it in a soup, and serves it to her dying mother.
    d. She agrees to stay away from her daughter forever.

12. In the story, what does An-mei learn from her own mother?
    a. She learns that one's love and respect for one's mother is deep within one's bones.
    b. She learns not to run away from home.
    c. She learns not to eat hot soup from a big kettle.
    d. She learns that under no circumstances should she ever quarrel with her uncle.

Joy Luck Club - Multiple Choice Quizzes - page 5

The Red Candle told by Lindo Jong

1. How did Lindo Jong become engaged to her future husband, Tyan-yu?
    a. He proposed to her after watching a romantic movie.
    b. A match was arranged through a matchmaker when Lindo was two and Tyan-yu was only one.
    c. Their mothers discussed their growing love and promised to let them marry.
    d. They decided to marry after going on many dates when they were in their teens.

2. How did Lindo first become a member of the Huang household?
    a. When she was twelve, her family moved away and sent her to live with the Huang family.
    b. When she needed a place to live, they graciously took her in.
    c. She applied for a position in their household.
    d. Tyan-yu asked his mother if Lindo could come and live with them.

3. What gift did Lindo's mother give to Lindo as the family moved away?
    a. a huge snake
    b. her **chang**, a necklace made out of a tablet of red jade
    c. a pair of diamond earrings
    d. an envelope full of money

4. How did Tyan-yu make Lindo cry the first night she lived in his house?
    a. He demanded that they make love.
    b. He complained that the soup was not hot enough, spilled the bowl as if it were an accident, waited until she sat down before demanding more rice, and asked why she had such an unpleasant face when looking at him.
    c. He told her that he had never loved her.
    d. He told her that she was way too fat for his liking.

5. What did Lindo's mother-in-law instruct the servants to teach Lindo?
    a. to be a good seamstress
    b. to perform a variety of household duties so that she would be a good wife
    c. how to choose low-fat foods for her husband
    d. how to lose weight by eating only fruit

6. What promise did Lindo make to herself on her wedding day?
    a. She promised herself that she would someday kill Tyan-yu.
    b. She promised herself that she would run away at the first opportunity.
    c. She promised herself that she would always remember her parents' wishes but would never forget herself.
    d. She promised herself that she would write to her parents and tell them that they had made a big mistake in letting her go.

Joy Luck Club - Multiple Choice Quizzes - page 6

7. Why was Lindo unafraid while she was led down a path on her wedding day?
    a. because she didn't know anyone who was present
    b. because she could see what was inside herself
    c. because her face was covered by a big scarf and she couldn't see enough to be afraid
    d. because she knew that her parents would come back for her

8. What was the red candle's significance and what was supposed to happen to it?
    a. It symbolized Lindo's marriage to Tyan-yu, and it was supposed to be lit at both ends and kept burning all night long.
    b. It was a symbol of the children she would bear, and it was supposed to burn out only after she and her husband made love.
    c. It symbolized fertility, and it was supposed to be kept burning always.
    d. It symbolized her fears, and it was supposed to make her keep trying to please Tyan-yu.

9. What lie did the matchmaker's servant tell?
    a. She said that Tyan-yu and Lindo were a good match.
    b. She said that the candle burned all night.
    c. She said that the candle burned out at just the right time.
    d. She said that she saw Lindo kissing another man in the garden.

10. What mark on Tyan-yu did Lindo use to "prove" her marriage was rotting?
    a. a big red welt on his cheek
    b. an ingrown toenail on his left foot
    c. a small black mole on his back
    d. a mysterious X written on her bedroom wall

11. How did Lindo escape from the marriage to Tyan-yu?
    a. She convinced them that the pregnant servant girl was really of imperial blood and was Tyan-yu's spiritual wife.
    b. She lied and said that she couldn't have children.
    c. She ran away when everyone else was at dinner.
    d. She killed Tyan-yu.

12. What is the significance in the story of the Festival of Pure Brightness?
    a. It is the day when Lindo carried out her plan and a day she still celebrates by taking off all her bracelets and remembering the day when she finally knew a genuine thought and could follow where it went.
    b. It was the day when she met her second husband, the man she really loved.
    c. It was the last time she could remember having a good time.
    d. It was the last time she saw her mother and father alive.

Joy Luck Club - Multiple Choice Quizzes - page 7

The Moon Lady told by Ying-ying St. Clair

1. What does Ying-yin say her earliest recollection is?
    a. hearing her father yell at her for disobeying him
    b. telling the Moon Lady her secret wish
    c. seeing the Moon Lady dance in the garden
    d. listening to her mother tell her about love

2. Why does the Amah tell Ying-ying that she must keep her wishes secret?
    a. because it is so much fun to have secrets that other people don't know
    b. because secrets are always kept during special festivals
    c. because girls are trained to keep secrets
    d. because if she tells her secret wish, it will no longer be a wish but become a selfish desire

3. How did Ying-ying wind up in the water?
    a. She was pushed by a mysterious stranger.
    b. While listening to the Moon Lady sing, she got dizzy and fell in.
    c. She fell off the back of the boat.
    d. Amah shoved her in for being bad.

4. What is the ultimate fate of the Moon Lady?
    a. to forever seek her own selfish wishes
    b. to have to live her life as a man
    c. to lose her voice and be unable to sing
    d. to become one of the lost ghosts of the village

5. What was the effect on Ying-ying of listening to the Moon Lady's story?
    a. She thought the story was silly.
    b. She cried and shook with despair.
    c. The story made her laugh.
    d. The story made her want to go home.

6. What does the Moon Lady represent for Ying-ying?
    a. an illusion, a wish granted that could not be trusted
    b. power, money, and fame
    c. the loss of love
    d. a way to become a star

Joy Luck Club - Multiple Choice Quizzes - page 8

7. What wish did Ying-ying ask for from the Moon Lady?
    a. to become a singing star
    b. to be found
    c. to be pretty
    d. to find her family again

8. How does Ying-ying's story reflect her life and that of her daughter?
    a. She says that she and her daughter are both lost.
    b. She says that she and her daughter could both have been stars.
    c. She feels that she and her daughter were destined to become singers.
    d. She feels that she and her daughter both could have played the role of the Moon Lady.

Joy Luck Club - Multiple Choice Quizzes - page 9

SECTION 2 - THE TWENTY-SIX MALIGNANT GATES

These stories address the mothers telling their daughters how to live. The daughters reject their mothers' ideas, but what the mothers say comes true. This point is symbolized in the mother who tells the daughter not to ride her bicycle around the corner because she will fall down and cry and not be heard by her mother. The daughter rejects the mother's ideas but then she jumps on her bicycle and falls even before she reaches the corner.

Rules of the Game told by Waverly Jong

1. What was "the art of invisible strength" that Waverly's mother taught her?
   a. It was a special strength that comes from angels.
   b. It was the strength that comes from lifting weights.
   c. It was a strategy for winning arguments and gaining respect from others.
   d. It was a way of never losing even one chess tournament.

2. How did Waverly's mother demonstrate the art of invisible strength?
   a. She gave Waverly a gift of salted plums precisely because she kept quiet and didn't request them.
   b. She ignored Waverly and never praised her.
   c. She showed Waverly how muscular her body was getting.
   d. She remained silent for seven days straight.

3. How did Waverly learn to play expert chess?
   a. She took classes through a kind of community center.
   b. In the beginning she taught herself and then she played with Lau Po.
   c. Her brother Winston taught her.
   d. Her mother taught her.

4. What would Waverly's mother say when she attended Waverly's chess exhibition games outdoors?
   a. "Is my daughter the chess master."
   b. "Is funny game."
   c. "Is luck."
   d. "Chess is so silly."

5. Why did Waverly run away?
   a. She ran away because her mother was embarrassing her and showing off.
   b. She was tired of being made to play in chess tournaments.
   c. She had told her mother that the next time she didn't get her own way, she would run away.
   d. She felt that her skills as a great chess player weren't being appreciated properly.

Joy Luck Club - Multiple Choice Quizzes - page 10

6. How did Waverly's mother treat her when she returned home after running away?
    a. She was totally apologetic and gave Waverly anything she wanted.
    b. She talked with Waverly about solving her problems.
    c. She promised not to cause any more problems for Waverly.
    d. She treated her as though she didn't exist.

7. What was Waverly's mother's view of "rules"?
    a. She believed that people from foreign countries must learn the American "rules."
    b. She believed that the rules were a way of tricking foreigners into making mistakes.
    c. She believed that rules were made to be broken.
    d. She believed that rules applied to grownups but not to children.

8. At the end of the story, who is Waverly's imaginary chess opponent?
    a. Lau Po
    b. Her brother Winston
    c. Her father
    d. Her mother

Joy Luck Club - Multiple Choice Quizzes - page 11

The Voice from the Wall told by Lena St. Clair

1. What does the dead beggar say when he returns?
    a. I wish I had not gone away.
    b. The worst is on the other side.
    c. I have come back for revenge.
    d. I never was a good person before.

2. How did the American immigration authorities categorize Lena's mother?
    a. as a "displaced person."
    b. as a troublesome foreigner
    c. as an Asian of unknown origin
    d. as a female Oriental

3. Why does Lena want to know "the worst possible thing that can happen" to her?
    a. so that she can avoid it
    b. so that she can be frightened once and for all
    c. so that she can understand her life better
    d. so that she can know as many bad things as her mother does

4. Why did Lena start telling lies?
    a. She started telling lies in order to get her own way.
    b. She started telling lies to prevent bad things from happening in the future.
    c. She started telling lies to make additional money.
    d. She started telling lies to get the best of her mother.

5. What was Lena's great hope when the family moved out of Oakland?
    a. She hoped that she would become famous.
    b. She hoped that her mother would leave.
    c. She hoped that her father would get medical help for her mother.
    d. She hoped that she might be able to leave all the old fears behind.

6. What did Lena hear through the wall of the new apartment?
    a. the sound of mice running around
    b. the mother and daughter next door arguing
    c. the woman next door reciting poetry in Chinese
    d. the mother and father next door talking to each other

7. Why did the girl from next door leave her own apartment?
    a. because she was tired of having to stay inside
    b. because her mother kicked her out
    c. because she wanted to get out to see her boyfriend
    d. because she was curious about how Lena and her family lived

Joy Luck Club - Multiple Choice Quizzes - page 12

8. How did the girl from next door get out of Lena's bedroom?
   a. She climbed out onto the fire escape and back into her own apartment.
   b. She climbed out onto a very tall tree.
   c. She just went downstairs and out the front door.
   d. She jumped out of a window onto a soft awning below.

9. What happened later that night after the girl and her mother had argued?
   a. The girl and her mother cried and laughed and shouted with love.
   b. The mother had the girl taken away by the police.
   c. The mother came over to talk to Lena.
   d. The mother called to ask Lena if she had seen her daughter.

10. What hope did Lena have after watching the girl next door with her mother?
    a. She hoped that she and her mother could get to know the people next door.
    b. She hoped that her father would allow her to have a boyfriend too.
    c. She hoped that the girl would visit her again soon.
    d. She hoped that things could be better than they appeared.

Joy Luck Club - Multiple Choice Quizzes - page 13

Half and Half told by Rose Hsu Jordan

1. What did Rose's mother used to carry to church services at the First Chinese Baptist Church?
    a. a hymnal
    b. a big heavy black Bible
    c. a small leatherette Bible
    d. a small picture of her dead parents

2. What makes Rose sure that her mother knows the Bible is still under a table leg in her kitchen?
    a. because her mother mentions it often
    b. because her mother is not the greatest housekeeper and yet the Bible is still clean white after twenty years
    c. because the Bible is there in plain sight
    d. because she has caught her mother reading it

3. How did the decision making start and then change in Rose's marriage?
    a. At first she decided everything but then her husband took over.
    b. At first her husband decided everything but then he lost a malpractice lawsuit and wanted her to make all of the decisions for them.
    c. At first she and her husband decided everything equally but then he wouldn't let her make any decisions.
    d. At first they voted on everything but later they drew straws to see who would get to make a decision.

4. What did Rose find out "faith" was?
    a. an illusion that somehow one is in control
    b. just God's way of fooling people
    c. simply a way of pretending
    d. a silly way of behaving that Chinese people engage in

5. What was the name of Rose's mother's little Chinese book and what was in it?
    a. **Foolish Chinese Children and Their Parents** showed how parents had failed their children by coddling them
    b. **Wickedness in Children** told stories of very young children who were evil.
    c. **The Twenty-six Malignant Gates** showed how children are predisposed to certain dangers on certain days based on their Chinese birthdates.
    d. **Drowned Children in America** which had pictures in it of children who had drowned after coming to America to live

Joy Luck Club - Multiple Choice Quizzes - page 14

6. What did Rose and her mother do early on the morning after Rose's brother drowned?
   a. They prayed at the First Chinese Baptist Church.
   b. They spent the morning confessing their sins.
   c. They went back to the beach to try to find him.
   d. They yelled at each other and accused each other of being responsible for his death.

7. Why did Rose's mother throw her blue sapphire ring into the water?
   a. because blue was the same color as the water
   b. because she thought it would divert the Coiling Dragon so that he would release her son from the water
   c. because she thought God would exchange her son for the ring
   d. because she felt guilty having such a beautiful ring after she had let her son drown

8. Why did Rose's mother throw an inner tube attached to a fishing pole into the water?
   a. She believed it would locate her lost son.
   b. She just couldn't think of anything else to do.
   c. She believed that Chinese fishermen had used the same technique.
   d. She thought that Bing would respond to the gadget.

9. When her mother gave up finding Bing, what emotion did Rose feel?
   a. absolute joy
   b. great sorrow
   c. relief
   d. blinding anger

10. When Rose took the Bible out from under the table leg, what did she find written in it?
    a. her mother's confession to God about losing her son
    b. her mother's angry statements about the death
    c. her brother's name written in it in erasable pencil under "Deaths"
    d. just a small notation about her brother in the back written in blue ink

Joy Luck Club - Multiple Choice Quizzes - page 15

Two Kinds told by Jing-mei Woo
1. What made Jing-mei's mother think that Jing-mei could be a prodigy?
    a. She thought anyone could be anything they wanted to be in America.
    b. Jing-mei had showed great promise when she was very young.
    c. An-Mei Hsu had mentioned that she thought Jing-mei was talented.
    d. She believed that anyone could accomplish greatness through prayer.

2. What did Jing-mei's mother lose in China?
    a. her mother and father, her family home, her first husband, and her twin baby daughters
    b. her honor
    c. her sense of humor
    d. her spirit

3. How did Jing-mei first envision herself as a prodigy?
    a. as a kind of Shirley Temple type
    b. as a celebrity on the Ed Sullivan show
    c. as a tap dancing Asian girl
    d. as a dainty ballerina, the Christ child, or Cinderella

4. What would perfection have meant for Jing-mei while she was waiting to become a prodigy?
    a. that her parents would adore her, she would be beyond reproach, and she would never feel the need to sulk for anything
    b. going to college
    c. learning to play chess
    d. just being left alone by her overly ambitious mother

5. Why did Jing-mei's mother read so many magazines?
    a. She read them to find stories of remarkable children.
    b. She read them to learn about how to raise children.
    c. She read them so that she could teach herself the English language.
    d. She read them so that she would feel like an educated American citizen.

6. What happened to all of Jing-mei's mother's early efforts to find out what kind of prodigy Jing-mei should be?
    a. They failed totally.
    b. They cost too much money.
    c. They were discarded when Jing-mei refused to try to achieve greatness.
    d. They didn't come true because she didn't pray hard enough

Joy Luck Club - Multiple Choice Quizzes - page 16

7. What was wrong with Jing-mei's piano teacher and how did his defect affect her playing?
   a. He couldn't read music, so he didn't know if she was playing the right notes.
   b. He was tone deaf, so he couldn't tell if she was playing in tune or not.
   c. He was deaf, so he couldn't even hear the notes she was playing.
   d. He had a huge dislike for little girl pianists, so he wouldn't have liked anything she played.

8. What piece did Jing-mei select for the talent show in the church hall?
   a. a piece called "Pleading Child"
   b. a special Christmas piece
   c. a piece called "I Have Talent"
   d. a particularly difficult piece to play

9. Who was the only person in the church hall who thought Jing-mei's performance was good?
   a. her mother
   b. her father
   c. Waverly Jong
   d. her piano teacher

10. What did Jing-mei realize after she had played both "Pleading Child" and "Perfectly Contented" a few times?
    a. that it too was beautiful
    b. that the two pieces were two halves of the same song
    c. that the latter was very difficult to play
    d. that "Perfectly Contented" made her feel better about her mother's death

Joy Luck Club - Multiple Choice Quizzes - page 17

AMERICAN TRANSLATION

The stories in this section continue the clash between the values of the Chinese mothers and the new lives embraced by the American daughters. This is symbolized in the mirrored armoire in the master suite of the daughter's new condominium. It's mirrors are at the foot of the bed and will reflect happiness away from the daughter. The mother placed a gilt-edged mirror on the headboard of the bed to bring the daughter "peach-blossom luck," fertility, the grandchildren that the grandmother-to-be desires.

Rice Husband told by Lena St. Clair
1. What does the saying, "If the lips are gone, the teeth will be cold," mean?
   a. that dental problems never go away
   b. that one thing is always the result of another
   c. that it is best not to have dental surgery
   d. that nothing in this life is easy

2. What does Lena's mother see?
   a. She sees the bad things that will affect her family.
   b. She sees back into the past and far into the future.
   c. She sees only positive coming events.
   d. She sees the best in everyone she meets.

3. What are the three things that Lena's mother predicted that came true?
   a. a grocery store that burned down, an illness that kept Lena in bed for weeks, and Lena's father's death
   b. that Lena and two of her female cousins would get divorced
   c. her family's falling into debt, a great financial reversal on the horizon, and Lena's marriage
   d. a miscarriage, a bank failure, and Lena's father's death

4. What does Lena think her mother will see during her visit with her and Harold?
   a. how ugly their cat is
   b. how wrong Lena and Harold are for each other
   c. how boring Lena's life is
   d. how poorly built Lena's house is

5. What physical aspect of Lena's house does her mother connect with a feeling?
   a. the slant of the floor that makes her feel as if she is "running down"
   b. the placement of the mirrors makes her feel lonely
   c. the windows that need repainting make her feel doomed
   d. the height of the windows that make her feel angry

Joy Luck Club - Multiple Choice Quizzes - page 18

6. What food does Harold not realize that Lena doesn't eat?
    a. bananas
    b. tomatoes
    c. ice cream
    d. whole wheat bread

7. Why does Harold hate it when Lena cries?
    a. He thinks it's manipulative.
    b. It makes him feel guilty.
    c. It makes him want to cry too.
    d. He thinks she fakes her feelings.

8. Why does the marble end table collapse?
    a. It collapses because it is not sturdy.
    b. It collapses because Lena's mother puts too much weight on it.
    c. It collapses mysteriously for no reason at all.
    d. It collapses because Harold bumps into it.

9. When Lena says, "I knew it would happen," what question does her mother ask?
    a. "How could you possibly know that?"
    b. "I don't think you could have known."
    c. "Then why you don't stop it?"
    d. "Why do you do such dumb things, then?"

Four Directions told by Waverly Jong

1. What did Waverly want to tell her mother at lunch?
    a. She wanted to tell her mother that she was going on a special diet.
    b. She wanted to tell her mother that she was getting married again.
    c. She wanted to tell her mother that she was getting divorced.
    d. She wanted to tell her mother that she was pregnant.

2. What did Waverly's mother do when she found that Waverly had eloped with her first husband?
    a. She yelled at them for hours.
    b. She threw her shoe at them.
    c. She threatened the man's life.
    d. She told them never to come to see her again.

3. Why did Waverly first stop playing chess as a child?
    a. because she felt her mother was trying to take all the credit for her winning
    b. because she was terribly bored
    c. because she wanted to stop while she was ahead
    d. because she felt she had outgrown the game

4. What special thing could Waverly's mother do to change Waverly's view of a person?
    a. She could make Waverly see each of the person's traits in a new, negative way.
    b. She could make even weak people seem strong in Waverly's eyes?
    c. She could tell Waverly that they looked like someone she had disliked in her childhood.
    d. She could tell lies so convincingly that Waverly no longer knew who she liked.

5. What mistake did Rich make about the wine at the dinner with Waverly's family?
    a. He got very drunk at dinner.
    b. He drank right out of the bottle.
    c. He served red wine instead of white wine.
    d. He drank two full glasses while everybody else had a half-inch "just for taste."

6. Why was Waverly so anxious that her mother was the queen while she, Waverly, was the pawn?
    a. because then Waverly could only run away while her mother could move in all directions
    b. because she hated to think that her mother could be royalty
    c. because she had once dreamt that she was just a pawn
    d. because in her last tournament game she lost a pawn

Joy Luck Club - Multiple Choice Quizzes - page 20

7. In what way was Waverly confused about where her mother came from?
    a. She thought her mother was from Shanghai, but she was really from Canton.
    b. She thought that her mother was American born when really she was born in China.
    c. She thought her mother was born in China when really she was born right in San Francisco
    d. She thought her mother was born in **Taiwan**, but her mother was really born in **Taiyuan**.

8. What trip is Waverly contemplating at the end of the story and with whom would she travel?
    a. She is contemplating a trip to Taiwan.
    b. She is contemplating a cruise to Bermuda.
    c. She is contemplating a trip to China made by herself, her mother, and Rich.
    d. She is contemplating a trip to China with just Rich and Shoshana.

Without Wood told by Rose Hsu Jordan
1. When Rose was little, what did she believe?
    a. She believed a mirror could see only her face but that her mother could see her inside out even when Rose was not in the room.
    b. She believed in the Chinese equivalent of Santa Clause.
    c. She believed in all kinds of ghosts.
    d. She believed that her mother was immortal.

2. Why did Rose's mother say that Rose was "without wood"?
    a. She explained that Rose was confused all of the time because she listened to too many people.
    b. She said that everything in Rose's house was made of plastic.
    c. She thought that Rose had no appreciation for antique wood furniture.
    d. She thought that Rose was so slender that she had no central core.

3. Why did Rose stay in bed for three days?
    a. because her husband had left her and she was unable to make the simplest decisions
    b. because she had a bad case of food poisoning
    c. because she was very ill with a migraine headache
    d. because she couldn't get over her uncle's death

4. Where did Rose tell Ted she was going to live?
    a. She said she was going to continue to live in the house they had shared while they were married.
    b. She said that she was moving into a hotel.
    c. She said that she was going home to live with her mother.
    d. She said that she was going into a nunnery.

5. When Rose says that Ted is **hulihudu**, what does she mean?
    a. that he is wicked
    b. that he is weak
    c. that he is confused
    d. that is extremely stupid

6. What does Rose's mother plant in Rose's garden?
    a. daffodils
    b. weeds
    c. violets
    d. petunias

Joy Luck Club - Multiple Choice Quizzes - page 22

Best Quality told by Jing-mei Woo

1. What is Jing-mei's "life's importance" gift from her mother?
    a. a jade pendant on a gold chain
    b. a special locket with her mother's hair in it
    c. a diary to keep her most important thoughts in
    d. a diamond brooch

2. Why did Jing-mei's mother not want to keep the crab that had lost a leg?
    a. because a missing leg on a crab is a bad sign on a Chinese New Year
    b. because the crab was too small to keep anyway
    c. because she felt sorry for the crab and didn't want to eat it
    d. because she once ate a crab without a leg and got sick from it

3. Why did Jing-mei leave the room while the crabs were being steamed?
    a. She left the room because she got tired of talking to her mother.
    b. She left the room because her mother was making her so angry.
    c. She left the room because she could not bear to remain while the crabs died.
    d. She left the room because she was tired and didn't feel like helping with dinner.

4. How do Jing-mei and her mother disagree in regard to Waverly Jong?
    a. Jing-mei likes Waverly a lot, but her mother has never liked Waverly.
    b. Jing-mei thinks Waverly is pretty, but her mother thinks she is ugly.
    c. Jing-mei admires her while her mother says that Waverly is like a crab, always walking sideways, moving crooked.
    d. Jing-mei thinks that Waverly always tells the truth, but once her mother caught Waverly in a lie.

5. How did Waverly insult Jing-mei professionally?
    a. She said that her firm had decided that Jing-mei's freelance work was unacceptable.
    b. She mentioned that she thought Jing-mei's work was messy.
    c. She said that Jing-mei had never been able to spell correctly.
    d. She said that Jing-mei didn't dress well at work.

6. Who got the crab with the missing leg?
    a. Waverly Jong
    b. Jing-mei's father
    c. Jing-mei
    d. Jing-mei's mother

Joy Luck Club - Multiple Choice Quizzes - page 23

QUEEN MOTHER OF THE WESTERN SKIES

This series of stories represent the Chinese mothers trying to pass along the message that the daughters should lose their innocence but not their hope. This is symbolized by the woman teasing her baby granddaughter and remembering how she went from freedom and innocence and laughter to learning to protect herself. She taught her daughter to protect herself by shedding her own innocence. Now, seeing the laughing baby, the grandmother wonders if her daughter can learn through the child to keep her hope and to laugh forever.

Magpies told by An-mei Hsu

1. In what way does An-mei say that all people born girls are alike?
    a. They all can give birth to babies.
    b. Men take advantage of all of them.
    c. None of them has any sense.
    d. They are all like stairs, one step after another, going up and down, but all going the same way.

2. What did it mean to An-mei to be raised "the Chinese way"?
    a. It meant being taught to desire nothing, to swallow other people's misery, and to eat one's own bitterness.
    b. It meant learning to honor one's mother and father.
    c. It meant understanding how to sacrifice.
    d. It meant not having to say one is sorry.

3. How did An-mei's mother dishonor her widowhood?
    a. She married a much wealthier man than her first husband.
    b. She married a man with the same first name as her first husband.
    c. She married a man of whom her entire family disapproved.
    d. She became the third concubine to a rich man.

4. What did the turtle in the pond do to An-mei's tears?
    a. The turtle laughed at her tears.
    b. The turtle ate her tears.
    c. The turtle drowned in her tears.
    d. The turtle cringed and shook off her tears.

5. What happened to the eggs that poured out of the turtle's beak?
    a. They became birds.
    b. They fell to the ground and smashed.
    c. They turned into magic balls.
    d. They rose into the air and turned into smoke.

Joy Luck Club - Multiple Choice Quizzes - page 24

6. What emotion is usually associated with the magpies?
   a. anger
   b. sorrow
   c. elation
   d. joy

7. What did the turtle tell An-mei's mother as he drifted back into the pond?
   a. He told her not to remarry.
   b. He told her to be kind to her mother.
   c. He told her that it is useless to cry.
   d. He told her to go home to her family.

8. How did An-mei learn not to listen to something meaningless calling to her?
   a. by learning to ignore the loud sound of the clock on her bedroom wall
   b. by meditating for hours at a time
   c. by praying for guidance
   d. by wearing earplugs during the day

9. Why did An-mei's mother send An-mei out of their bedroom at night?
   a. because the bed was too small for two people
   b. because she felt that An-mei should learn to sleep alone
   c. because Wu Tsing had arrived and wanted to be with her
   d. because she tired of hearing An-mei's complaints

10. Why did An-mei's mother become Wu Tsing's concubine?
    a. She did it to make her family angry.
    b. She did it to get back at her mother for neglecting her.
    c. She did it because he paid her a vast sum of money.
    d. He raped her, thus giving her no choice but to stay with him as his concubine.

11. How did An-mei's mother die?
    a. She poisoned herself.
    b. She stabbed herself to death.
    c. She had a heart attack.
    d. She died of grief.

12. What promise did Wu Tsing make to An-mei's mother after she died?
    a. He said that he would raise her son and daughter at his honored children.
    b. He said that he would always think well of her.
    c. He said that he would support her father in his old age.
    d. He said that he would have her buried in a special burial plot.

13. What does An-mei say that her daughter's psychiatrist is?
    a. just another bird drinking from Rose's misery
    b. a quack
    c. a nice woman but not very bright
    d. a money grubber

14. How did the tired Chinese peasants get rid of the birds that were drinking their tears and eating their seeds?
    a. They prayed that they would go away.
    b. They chanted and meditated.
    c. They clapped their hands and shouted.
    d. They put away all of the food and water that the birds were eating and drinking.

Waiting Between the Trees told by Ying-ying St. Clair

1. How has Lena St. Clair unknowingly insulted her mother by giving her the guest bedroom in her home?
    a. The guest bedroom should be the biggest and best bedroom, but Lena's guest bedroom is tiny.
    b. The room faced south and frightened her mother.
    c. The room was decorated in red, an insulting color to an older Chinese woman.
    d. The room was too big for one small, older lady.

2. What did Lena do when she was born?
    a. She cried right away.
    b. She made her mother feel sick.
    c. She squirmed around so that the nurse had to hold onto her.
    d. She sprang from her mother like a slippery fish.

3. When Ying-ying was a young girl in Wushi, she was **lihai**? What does that mean?
    a. It means that she was wicked.
    b. It means that she was wild and stubborn.
    c. It means that she loved to read.
    d. It means that her parents were uneducated.

4. When did Ying-ying begin to know things before they happened?
    a. the night her aunt got married when Ying-ying was sixteen
    b. when she was around thirty
    c. when she got pregnant with her daughter
    d. when her husband beat her up

5. What sign happened to convince Ying-ying that she would marry the man who was a guest at her house?
    a. A large wind blew in from the north and the flower on the table nearby split from its stem and fell at her feet.
    b. She had a dream that contained every detail of the marriage.
    c. He winked at her and she just knew what would follow.
    d. She had always expected a tall, thin man would propose to her and the guest at her house was tall and thin.

6. Why did Ying-ying's husband leave her?
    a. He left her because she was boring to him.
    b. He left her to live with an opera singer.
    c. She got sick and he didn't want to live with a sick woman.
    d. She got pregnant and he didn't want any children.

7. What is the difference between what Lena sees in her mother and what her mother really is?
   a. Lena sees a Chinese woman, but her mother really is an American.
   b. Lena sees a dumb woman, but her mother really is smart.
   c. Lena sees a short person, but her mother is a tall person in her heart.
   d. Lena sees a small old lady, but Ying-ying really is a tiger lady.

8. Why, according to Ying-ying, is the tiger gold and black?
   a. because the gold side leaps with its fierce heart while the black side stands still with cunning and patience
   b. because the gold side is evil while the black side is good
   c. because it would be silly to have a blue and pink tiger
   d. because the gold is beautiful and complements the black

9. Why does Ying-ying abort her first child?
   a. because she is afraid she will die giving birth
   b. because she has no money to support the child
   c. because the child is going to be sickly
   d. because she hates her husband, the child's father

10. What did Ying-ying do for ten years at the country home of her cousin's family?
    a. She waited for a husband to come along.
    b. She waited between the trees.
    c. She worked as a maid.
    d. She learned to perform many wifely chores.

11. What did Ying-ying give up when she married St. Clair?
    a. her free will
    b. her money
    c. her child
    d. her spirit

12. At the end of the story, what does Ying-ying want to do for her daughter?
    a. She wants to give her daughter a lot of money.
    b. She wants to build a new house for her daughter.
    c. She wants to find her daughter a new husband.
    d. She wants to give her daughter her own spirit.

Joy Luck Club - Multiple Choice Quizzes - page 28

Double Face told by Lindo Jong
1. Why does Waverly Jong want to go to China?
    a. She wants to be among other people who look like her.
    b. She wants to escape the boredom of San Francisco.
    c. She wants to go to please her mother.
    d. She wants to go there for her second honeymoon.

2. Why does Waverly especially want to be Chinese?
    a. because she enjoys her heritage
    b. because it is so fashionable
    c. because she is marrying a Chinese man
    d. because she wants her daughter to also be Chinese

3. Why could Lindo's children not have American circumstances and Chinese character?
    a. because the two things do not mix
    b. because they have minds of their own
    c. because they have American character and Chinese circumstances instead
    d. because God willed it not to be so

4. Who first taught Lindo about America?
    a. a concubine
    b. a Chinese actor
    c. her husband
    d. an American-raised Chinese girl in Peking

5. What kind of job did Lindo get in the cookie factory?
    a. She got a job in a shop.
    b. She got a job driving a taxi.
    c. She got a job forming Chinese fortune cookies out of hot dough.
    d. She got a job as a waitress in a Chinese restaurant.

6. What was the fortune inside the cookie that Lindo gave to Tin?
    a. "Hi Handsome!"
    b. "A house is not home when a spouse is not at home."
    c. "Give me a call when you can."
    d. "I am lonely and available."

joy Luck Club - Multiple Choice Quizzes - page 29

7. Why does Waverly like the fact that she and her mother have crooked noses?
    a. just because she likes to look like her mother
    b. because she likes to look different
    c. because she thinks they make her and her mother look devious or two-faced
    d. just because it is their only flaw

8. At the end of the story, what is Lindo wondering about?
    a. She is wondering what she has lost in coming to America and what she has gotten back in return.
    b. She is wondering who her daughter will marry next.
    c. She is wondering how much it will cost to find a husband for her daughter.
    d. She is wondering what's for dinner.

A Pair of Tickets told by Jing-mei Woo

1. Why does Jing-mei feel different as her train leaves the Hong Kong border and enters Shenzhen, China?
    a. because she is becoming Chinese
    b. because she can no longer speak the dialect of the region she is in
    c. because her mother always talked about crossing that border
    d. because the air is somewhat lighter in Shenzhen

2. Where is Jing-mei meeting her two half-sisters?
    a. She is meeting them in Shanghai.
    b. She is meeting them in Oakland.
    c. She is meeting them in Canton.
    d. She is meeting them in Kweilin.

3. How did the half-sisters learn that their mother was dead?
    a. Somehow they just knew.
    b. They learned that their mother was dead when Auntie Lindo wrote a letter to them as Jing-mei asked her to do.
    c. Jing-mei phoned them weeks before her visit to China.
    d. Jing-mei's father secretly wrote to them so that they wouldn't have false expectations.

4. How did Jing-mei learn the details of what happened to her half-sisters?
    a. from her father
    b. from her mother's journals
    c. from Auntie Lindo
    d. from the half-sisters themselves

5. Why did Jing-mei's mother actually leave the babies?
    a. because she tired of carrying them
    b. because they wouldn't have been Chinese if she had brought them to America with her
    c. because she thought she was going to die and didn't want them to die with her
    d. because she traded them for a lot of money

6. Who found the babies?
    a. an old peasant woman
    b. a gypsy queen
    c. the mayor of a nearby town
    d. a large magical dog

7. What are the two different Chinese meanings of Suyuan, Jing-mei's mother's name?
    a. "Wonderful Mother" and "Honorable Adversary"
    b. "Good Wife" and "Nagging Woman"
    c. "Beautiful One" and "Light of My Life"
    d. "Long Cherished Wish" and "Long-Held Grudge"

8. What are the meanings of Jing-mei's name?
    a. "Just pure essence" and "younger sister
    b. "Sweet person" and "Loyal follower"
    c. "Loved relation" and "Beautiful dreamer"
    d. "Her Mother's Wish" and "Difficult Child"

ANSWER KEY: MULTIPLE CHOICE QUIZZES - *Joy Luck Club*

Joy Luck Club	*Scar*	*Candle*	*Moon*	*26 Gates*	*Voice*
1. B	1. C	1. B	1. B	1. C	1. B
2. D	2. A	2. A	2. D	2. A	2. A
3. D	3. B	3. B	3. C	3. B	3. A
4. A	4. B	4. B	4. A	4. C	4. B
5. C	5. A	5. B	5. B	5. A	5. D
6. B	6. B	6. C	6. A	6. D	6. B
7. A	7. D	7. B	7. B	7. A	7. B
8. B	8. C	8. A	8. A	8. D	8. A
9. C	9. B	9. B			9. A
10. B	10. A	10. C			10. D
	11. C	11. A			
	12. A	12. A			

Half & Half	*Two Kinds*	*Rice Husband*	*Four Directions*	*Without Wood*
1. C	1. A	1. B	1. B	1. A
2. B	2. A	2. A	2. B	2. A
3. B	3. D	3. D	3. A	3. A
4. A	4. A	4. B	4. A	4. A
5. C	5. A	5. A	5. D	5. C
6. C	6. A	6. C	6. A	6. B
7. B	7. C	7. A	7. D	
8. A	8. A	8. A	8. C	
9. D	9. D	9. C		
10. C	10. B			

Best Quality	*Magpies*	*Waiting*	*Double Face*	*Pair of Tickets*
1. A	1. D	1. A	1. D	1. A
2. A	2. A	2. D	2. B	2. A
3. C	3. D	3. B	3. A	3. B
4. C	4. B	4. A	4. D	4. A
5. A	5. A	5. A	5. C	5. C
6. D	6. D	6. B	6. B	6. A
	7. C	7. D	7. C	7. D
	8. A	8. A	8. A	8. A
	9. C	9. D		
	10. D	10. B		
	11. A	11. D		
	12. A	12. D		
	13. A			
	14. C			

PRE-READING VOCABULARY WORKSHEETS

VOCABULARY - *The Joy Luck Club*

The Joy Luck Club
Part I: Using Prior Knowledge and Contextual Clues
Below are the sentences in which the vocabulary words appear in the text. Read the sentence. Use any clues you can find in the sentence combined with your prior knowledge, and write what you think the bold words mean in the space provided.

1. And when I arrived, I realized how **shabby** my dreams were, how poor my thoughts.

2. When the sirens cried out to warn us of bombers, my neighbors and I jumped to our feet and **scurried** to the deep caves to hide like wild animals.

3. "What fine food we treated ourselves to with our **meager** allowances!"

4. What was worse, we asked among ourselves, to sit and wait for our own deaths with proper **somber** faces?

5. After everybody votes **unanimously** for the Canada gold stock, I go into the kitchen to ask Auntie An-mei why the Joy Luck Club started investing in stocks.

6. The white chenille bedspreads are so worn they are almost **translucent**.

7. At first my mother tried to **cultivate** some hidden genius in me.

8. And I am embarrassed by the end-of-the-year-banquet lie my aunties have told to mask their **generosity**.

Part II: Determining the Meaning -- Match the vocabulary words to their dictionary definitions.

___ 1. shabby   A. small or deficient in quantity
___ 2. scurried   B. allowing some light to pass through
___ 3. meager   C. of substandard quality
___ 4. somber   D. willingness to give; giving
___ 5. unanimously   E. completely in agreement
___ 6. translucent   F. grow; encourage; promote
___ 7. cultivate   G. serious
___ 8. generosity   H. scampered; went quickly with light steps

Joy Luck Club - Vocabulary - page 2

Scar

Part I: Using Prior Knowledge and Contextual Clues

Below are the sentences in which the vocabulary words appear in the text. Read the sentence. Use any clues you can find in the sentence combined with your prior knowledge, and write what you think the bold words mean in the space provided.

1. Many times Popo said aloud to all who could hear that my brother and I had fallen out of the **bowels** of a stupid goose, two eggs that nobody wanted, not even good enough to crack over rice porridge.

2. So you see, to Popo we were also very **precious.**

3. One day this bad girl shook her head so **vigorously** to refuse her auntie's simple request that a little white ball fell from her ear and out poured all her brains, as clear as chicken broth.

4. So when my brother gave her a sour look, Auntie said our mother was so thoughtless she had fled north in a big hurry, without taking the **dowry** furniture from her marriage to my father, without bringing her ten pairs of silver chopsticks, without paying respect to my father's grave and those of our ancestors.

5. When my brother accused Auntie of frightening our mother away, Auntie shouted that our mother had married a man named Wu Tsing who already had a wife, two **concubines,** and other bad children.

6. She looked strange, too, like the missionary ladies at our school who were **insolent** and bossy in their too-tall shoes, foreign clothes, and short hair.

7. That she seemed to float back and forth like a ghost, dipping cool cloths to lay on Popo's **bloated** face.

8. And because I remember Popo told me not to speak her name, I stood there, **mute**.

9. In the morning, Popo would use her sharp fingernails like tweezers and peel off the dead **membranes.**

Joy Luck Club - Vocabulary - page 3

Scar

Part II: Determining the Meaning -- Match the vocabulary words to their dictionary definitions.

___ 1. bowels   A. money or property brought by a bride to her husband
___ 2. precious   B. cherished; having value; beloved
___ 3. vigorously   C. thin layer of tissue
___ 4. dowry   D. arrogant; presumptuous and insulting
___ 5. concubines   E. speechless
___ 6. insolent   F. done with force or energy
___ 7. bloated   G. secondary wives
___ 8. mute   H. intestines; insides; guts
___ 9. membranes   I. swelled up

Joy Luck Club - Vocabulary - page 4

The Red Candle

Part I: Using Prior Knowledge and Contextual Clues

Below are the sentences in which the vocabulary words appear in the text. Read the sentence. Use any clues you can find in the sentence combined with your prior knowledge, and write what you think the bold words mean in the space provided.

1. She is crying with a **genuine** feeling and he says, "Promise! Promise! Honey-sweetheart, my promise is as good as gold."

2. It was summertime, very hot and dusty outside, and I could hear **cicadas** crying in the yard.

3. And this is when Huang Taitai looked down at me with a cloudy face as though she could **penetrate** my thoughts and see my future intentions.

4. Inside, the house held a different kind of **pretense.**

5. She had even commissioned someone to write **felicitous** messages on red banners, as if my parents themselves had draped these decorations to congratulate me on my good luck.

6. They **invaded** Shansi province, as well as the provinces bordering us.

7. The next morning the matchmaker made her proud **declaration** in front of Tyan-yu, his parents, and myself.

8. "They knew you would not believe me," I said in a **remorseful** tone, "because they know I do not want to leave the comforts of my marriage."

9. By mid-morning they had dragged the matchmaker's servant over to our house and **extracted** her terrible confession.

Part II: Determining the Meaning -- Match the vocabulary words to their dictionary definitions.

___ 1. genuine   A. pierce; force into
___ 2. cicadas   B. entered by force to conquer
___ 3. penetrate   C. suitable; appropriate
___ 4. pretense   D. pulled out
___ 5. felicitous   E. insects that make high-pitched, droning sound
___ 6. invaded   F. regretful; sorrowful
___ 7. declaration   G. false appearance
___ 8. remorseful   H. real
___ 9. extracted   I. statement

Joy Luck Club - Vocabulary - page 5

The Moon Lady

Part I: Using Prior Knowledge and Contextual Clues
Below are the sentences in which the vocabulary words appear in the text. Read the sentence. Use any clues you can find in the sentence combined with your prior knowledge, and write what you think the bold words mean in the space provided.

1. Everything in the room smelled of wet grass **simmering** in the heat.

2. And so the stale heat still remained in the shadows behind the curtains, heating up the **acrid** smells of my chamber pot, seeping into my pillow, chafing the back of my neck and puffing up my cheeks, so that I awoke that morning with a restless complaint.

3. "The third word in the next line," explained Baba, "was worn off the slab, its meaning washed away by centuries of rain, almost lost to **posterity** forever."

4. Suddenly I saw a dragonfly with a large crimson body and **transparent** wings.

5. I climbed into the rickshaw with my mother in it, which displeased Amah, because this was **presumptuous** behavior on my part and also because Amah loved me better than her own.

6. Mama and the other ladies were already seated on benches around the **pavilion**, fanning themselves furiously and slapping the sides of each other's heads when mosquitoes landed.

7. But the excitement soon **waned**, and the afternoon seemed to pass like any other at home.

8. And loud clanks and hissing sounds **erupted** as once again the boat began to move.

9. Both of these things seemed an **illusion** to me, a wish granted that could not be trusted.

Part II: Determining the Meaning -- Match the vocabulary words to their dictionary definitions.

___ 1. simmering   A. clear
___ 2. acrid   B. decreased
___ 3. posterity   C. excessively forward
___ 4. transparent   D. future generations
___ 5. presumptuous   E. unpleasant to the taste or smell
___ 6. pavilion   F. cooking just below boiling point
___ 7. waned   G. false perception of reality
___ 8. erupted   H. a shelter open to the air
___ 9. illusion   I. became violently active; exploded

Joy Luck Club - Vocabulary - page 6

Rules of the Game
Part I: Using Prior Knowledge and Contextual Clues
Below are the sentences in which the vocabulary words appear in the text. Read the sentence. Use any clues you can find in the sentence combined with your prior knowledge, and write what you think the bold words mean in the space provided.

1. It was a **strategy** for winning arguments, respect from others, and eventually, though neither of us knew it at the time, chess games.

2. It was said that he once cured a woman dying of an ancestral curse that had **eluded** the best of American doctors.

3. Inside, the butchers with their bloodstained white smocks **deftly** gutted the fish while customers cried out their orders and shouted, "Give me your freshest," to which the butchers always protested, "All are freshest."

4. My mother graciously thanked the unknown **benefactor**, saying, "Too good. Cost too much."

5. "Throw sand from the East to **distract** him."

6. I was still some 429 points away from grand-master status, but I was **touted** as the Great American Hope, a child prodigy and a girl to boot.

7. I was playing in a large high school auditorium that echoed with **phlegmy** coughs and the squeaky rubber knobs of chair legs sliding across freshly waxed wooden floors.

8. He wore a dark, **malodorous** suit.

9. My parents made many **concessions** to allow me to practice.

Part II: Determining the Meaning -- Match the vocabulary words to their dictionary definitions.
___ 1. strategy   A. divert
___ 2. eluded   B. bad-smelling
___ 3. deftly   C. full of mucus
___ 4. benefactor   D. skillfully
___ 5. distract   E. one who gives aid, esp. financial aid
___ 6. touted   F. escaped the understanding of
___ 7. phlegmy   G. plan
___ 8. malodorous   H. compromises
___ 9. concessions   I. publicly praised

Joy Luck Club - Vocabulary - page 7

The Voice from the Wall

Part I: Using Prior Knowledge and Contextual Clues
Below are the sentences in which the vocabulary words appear in the text. Read the sentence. Use any clues you can find in the sentence combined with your prior knowledge, and write what you think the bold words mean in the space provided.

1. And it became so mysterious that I spent all my energies unraveling this door, until the day I was finally able to pry it open with my small fingers, only to immediately fall headlong into the dark **chasm**.

2. My father said they didn't have rules for dealing with the Chinese wife of a **Caucasian** citizen

3. In fact, as I watched her, she seemed quite happy, her two brown braids bouncing **jauntily** in rhythm to her walk.

4. And then she looked at me, in a strange way, as if she were begging me for her life, as if I could **pardon** her.

5. I opened the door **cautiously**, then swung it wide open with surprise.

6. Maybe she had listened through the wall and heard nothing, the **stagnant** silence of our unhappy house.

7. I was **stunned**.

8. I would watch my mother lying in her bed, **babbling** to herself as she sat on the sofa.

Part II: Determining the Meaning -- Match the vocabulary words to their dictionary definitions.
- ___ 1. chasm
- ___ 2. Caucasian
- ___ 3. jauntily
- ___ 4. pardon
- ___ 5. cautiously
- ___ 6. stagnant
- ___ 7. stunned
- ___ 8. babbling

A. having a buoyant or self-confident attitude
B. abyss; gorge; steep-sided hole
C. motionless
D. astounded; dazed
E. forgive
F. light-skinned; often a person of European descent
G. talking in nonsense
H. carefully

Joy Luck Club - Vocabulary - page 8

Half and Half

Part I: Using Prior Knowledge and Contextual Clues
Below are the sentences in which the vocabulary words appear in the text. Read the sentence. Use any clues you can find in the sentence combined with your prior knowledge, and write what you think the bold words mean in the space provided.

1. I think it's **ironic** that my mother wants me to fight the divorce.

2. Seventeen years ago she was **chagrined** when I started dating Ted.

3. When he pressed me, I told him what his mother had said, **verbatim,** without comment.

4. I preferred to ignore the world around me, **obsessing** only over what was in front of me: my T-square, my X-acto knife, my blue pencil.

5. He asked me to decide on the most **trivial** matters, as if he were baiting me.

6. Her hair, her clothes, they were all heavy with the cold water, but she stood quietly, calm and **regal** as a mermaid queen who had just arrived out of the sea.

7. And she would stand straight as a **sentinel,** until three times her eyesight failed her and Bing turned into a dark spot of churning seaweed.

8. The line became **taut** and she strained to hold on tight.

Part II: Determining the Meaning -- Match the vocabulary words to their dictionary definitions.
___ 1. ironic   A. of little importance
___ 2. chagrined   B. royal
___ 3. verbatim   C. guard
___ 4. obsessing   D. thinking continually about something
___ 5. trivial   E. tight
___ 6. regal   F. distressed; put out; ill at ease
___ 7. sentinel   G. word for word
___ 8. taut   H. contrary to what is expected

Joy Luck Club - Vocabulary - page 9

Two Kinds

Part I: Using Prior Knowledge and Contextual Clues
Below are the sentences in which the vocabulary words appear in the text. Read the sentence. Use any clues you can find in the sentence combined with your prior knowledge, and write what you think the bold words mean in the space provided.

1. We didn't immediately pick the right kind of **prodigy.**

2. I got so bored I started counting the **bellows** of the foghorns out on the bay while my mother drilled me in other areas.

3. She seemed entranced by the music, a little frenzied piano piece with this **mesmerizing** quality, sort of quick passages and then teasing lilting ones before it returned to the quick playful parts.

4. The girl had the **sauciness** of a Shirley Temple.

5. The little Chinese girl sat down also to play an **encore** of "Anitra's Dance" by Grieg.

6. So I never found a way to ask her why she had hoped for something so large that failure was **inevitable.**

Part II: Determining the Meaning -- Match the vocabulary words to their dictionary definitions.

___ 1. prodigy   A. hypnotizing
___ 2. bellows   B. quality of being impossible to control or repress
___ 3. mesmerizing   C. exceptional talents or person with exceptional talents
___ 4. sauciness   D. unavoidable; bound to happen
___ 5. encore   E. very loud, deep sounds
___ 6. inevitable   F. additional performance in response to the demand
                           of the audience

Joy Luck Club - Vocabulary - page 10

Rice Husband

Part I: Using Prior Knowledge and Contextual Clues
Below are the sentences in which the vocabulary words appear in the text. Read the sentence. Use any clues you can find in the sentence combined with your prior knowledge, and write what you think the bold words mean in the space provided.

1. But now she **laments** that she never did anything to stop them.

2. This would have been a funny incident to remember from my childhood, but it is actually a memory I recall from time to time with a mixture of nausea and **remorse.**

3. Their faces were covered with every kind of misery I could imagine: pits and pustules, cracks and bumps, and fissures that I was sure erupted with the same **vehemence** as snails writhing in a bed of salt.

4. He had just been accepted to Cal State Hayward and was planning to become a **podiatrist.**

5. And later, for several hours after that, I sat hunched on the fire escape landing outside my bedroom, **retching** back into the ice cream container.

6. Harold puts his magazine down, now wearing his open-mouthed **exasperated** look.

Part II: Determining the Meaning -- Match the vocabulary words to their dictionary definitions.
___ 1. laments   A. intensity
___ 2. remorse   B. regrets
___ 3. vehemence   C. at the end of patience; irritated
___ 4. podiatrist   D. feeling of regret for one's misdeeds or sins
___ 5. retching   E. vomiting
___ 6. exasperated   F. foot doctor

Joy Luck Club - Vocabulary - page 11

Four Directions

Part I: Using Prior Knowledge and Contextual Clues
Below are the sentences in which the vocabulary words appear in the text. Read the sentence. Use any clues you can find in the sentence combined with your prior knowledge, and write what you think the bold words mean in the space provided.

1. It was fashionable, yet not **radically** so.

2. "Nothing is wrong with my heart," she huffed as she kept a **disparaging** eye on the waiter.

3. And so I watched her, seeing her reaction to the changes in my apartment-from the **pristine** habitat I maintained after the divorce, when all of a sudden I had too much time to keep my life in order-to this present chaos, a home full of life and love.

4. I knew at exactly what point their faces would fall when my seemingly simple and childlike strategy would reveal itself as a devastating and **irrevocable** course.

5. Because the sponsors and the **benevolent** associations would start calling her, asking, shouting, pleading to make me play again

6. He made everyone laugh and his own laugh was deep, **sonorous,** masculinely sexy.

7. So that with him I was completely naked, and when I was feeling the most **vulnerable**-when the wrong word would have sent me flying out the door forever-he always said exactly the right thing at the right moment.

Part II: Determining the Meaning -- Match the vocabulary words to their dictionary definitions.

___ 1. radically   A. characterized by being or doing good
___ 2. disparaging   B. in perfect condition
___ 3. pristine   C. departing from the norm; extremely
___ 4. irrevocable   D. full, deep or rich in sound
___ 5. benevolent   E. can't be changed back
___ 6. sonorous   F. belittling
___ 7. vulnerable   G. able to be hurt

Joy Luck Club - Vocabulary - page 12

Without Wood

Part I: Using Prior Knowledge and Contextual Clues

Below are the sentences in which the vocabulary words appear in the text. Read the sentence. Use any clues you can find in the sentence combined with your prior knowledge, and write what you think the bold words mean in the space provided.

1. I had started to **inventory** the bookshelves when I got a letter from Ted, a note actually, written hurriedly in ballpoint on his prescription notepad.

2. And in almost every case, the American **version** was much better.

3. The big oak door that opens into a **foyer** filled with stained-glass windows.

4. And I knew he had done that, not out of any concern for me, but because when he wants something, he gets impatient and **irrational** about people who make him wait.

5. And then without missing a beat, he proceeded to say what he really wanted, which was more **despicable** than all the terrible things I had imagined.

6. Ted was shivering in his sports jacket as he **surveyed** the damage to the garden.

7. Others had **anchored** on the side of the house.

Part II: Determining the Meaning -- Match the vocabulary words to their dictionary definitions.

___ 1. inventory   A. deserving strong dislike; vile
___ 2. version   B. looked over
___ 3. foyer   C. not reasonable
___ 4. irrational   D. description or account from one point of view
___ 5. despicable   E. attached; held on to
___ 6. surveyed   F. take a count of
___ 7. anchored   G. entrance hall

Joy Luck Club - Vocabulary - page 13

Best Quality

Part I: Using Prior Knowledge and Contextual Clues
Below are the sentences in which the vocabulary words appear in the text. Read the sentence. Use any clues you can find in the sentence combined with your prior knowledge, and write what you think the bold words mean in the space provided.

1. It's as though we were all sworn to the same secret **covenant,** so secret we don't even know what we belong to.

2. Two years ago, she had tried to **evict** them on the pretext that relatives from China were coming to live there.

3. But the couple saw through her **ruse** to get around rent control.

4. Judging by his **preamble** of snorts and leg slaps, I figured he must have practiced this joke many times: "I tell my daughter, Hey, why be poor? Marry rich!"

5. Maybe I'm being **paranoid**, being a mother, but you just can't be too safe these days."

6. My father poked at the **remnants** of his crab.

7. I waited for her to **chastise** me.

Part II: Determining the Meaning -- Match the vocabulary words to their dictionary definitions.

___ 1. covenant A. introductory occurrence or statement
___ 2. evict B. agreement
___ 3. ruse C. left-overs
___ 4. preamble D. characterized by extreme fear or distrust of others
___ 5. paranoid E. to put out, throw out or expel
___ 6. remnants F. criticize; punish; reprimand
___ 7. chastise G. a crafty strategy or plan

Joy Luck Club - Vocabulary - page 14

Magpies

Part I: Using Prior Knowledge and Contextual Clues
Below are the sentences in which the vocabulary words appear in the text. Read the sentence. Use any clues you can find in the sentence combined with your prior knowledge, and write what you think the bold words mean in the space provided.

1. She told me about narrow streets with crowded **bazaars**.

2. My mother gave quick instructions to our **porter,** pointed to our two small trunks and handed him money, as if she had done this every day of her life.

3. Four posts held up a silk **canopy** and at each post dangled large silk ties holding back curtains.

4. This was a wonderful clock to see, but after I heard it that first hour, then the next, and then always, this clock became an **extravagant** nuisance.

5. She was looking behind at everyone with a **simpering** smile, as if they were there to honor her.

6. And two delicate slippers with the softest leather soles and two giant pearls on each toe, to light her way to **nirvana.**

7. He promised to **revere** her as if she had been First Wife, his only wife.

Part II: Determining the Meaning -- Match the vocabulary words to their dictionary definitions.
___ 1. bazaars   A. roof-like covering
___ 2. porter   B. place of perfect happiness
___ 3. canopy   C. treat with respect
___ 4. extravagant   D. person who carries baggage
___ 5. simpering   E. beyond necessary; luxurious
___ 6. nirvana   F. silly or self-conscious
___ 7. revere   G. street markets

Joy Luck Club - Vocabulary - page 15

Waiting Between the Trees
Part I: Using Prior Knowledge and Contextual Clues
Below are the sentences in which the vocabulary words appear in the text. Read the sentence. Use any clues you can find in the sentence combined with your prior knowledge, and write what you think the bold words mean in the space provided.

1. I wore a **smirk** on my face.

2. "His mother will treat you like a servant" **chided** one half-sister upon hearing the other's choice.

3. But I was too **vain** to think any one boy was good enough for me.

4. He had long **tapered** fingers, fat earlobes, and slick hair that rose high to reveal a large forehead.

5. Later still, when I overcame my grief and came to have nothing in my heart but **loathing** despair, my youngest aunt told me of others.

6. That I became **abandoned** goods.

7. The black side stands still with **cunning** hiding its gold between trees, seeing and not being seen, waiting patiently for things to come.

Part II: Determining the Meaning -- Match the vocabulary words to their dictionary definitions.
___ 1. smirk   A. gradually smaller from one end to the other
___ 2. chided   B. conceited; proud
___ 3. vain   C. deserted; left
___ 4. tapered   D. offensively self-satisfied smile
___ 5. loathing   E. great dislike
___ 6. abandoned   F. deceitful cleverness
___ 7. cunning   G. scold mildly to correct or improve

Joy Luck Club - Vocabulary - page 16

Double Face

Part I: Using Prior Knowledge and Contextual Clues
Below are the sentences in which the vocabulary words appear in the text. Read the sentence. Use any clues you can find in the sentence combined with your prior knowledge, and write what you think the bold words mean in the space provided.

1. Then he says something to my daughter that really displeases her: "It's **uncanny** how much you two look alike!"

2. Our **longevity** will be adequate, not cut off too soon, not so long we become a burden.

3. And next to the word OCCUPATION, I wrote *student of* **theology**.

4. I saw two **pagodas**, one on each side of the street, as though they were the entrance to a great Buddha temple.

5. It said, "A house is not home when a **spouse** is not at home."

6. "What is this word, '**devious**,'" I ask.

Part II: Determining the Meaning -- Match the vocabulary words to their dictionary definitions.
     1. uncanny   A. study of religion
     2. longevity   B. wife or husband
     3. theology   C. tall towers erected as a memorial or shrine
     4. pagodas   D. sneaky
     5. spouse   E. mysteriously strange
     6. devious   F. length of life

Joy Luck Club - Vocabulary - page 17

A Pair of Tickets

Part I: Using Prior Knowledge and Contextual Clues
Below are the sentences in which the vocabulary words appear in the text. Read the sentence. Use any clues you can find in the sentence combined with your prior knowledge, and write what you think the bold words mean in the space provided.

1. I don't know whether it's the **prospect** of seeing his aunt or if it's because he's back in China, but now he looks like he's a young boy, so innocent and happy I want to button his sweater and pat his head.

2. One minute she was talking to my father, complaining about the tenants upstairs, **scheming** how to evict them under the pretense that relatives from China were moving in.

3. And so they couldn't help but think of some miracle, some possible way of **reviving** her from the dead, so my mother could fulfill her dream.

4. "Oh, that must be Mama, no?" one of my sisters would whisper excitedly, pointing to another small woman completely **engulfed** in a tower of presents.

5. I see platforms crowded with people wearing **drab** Western clothes, with spots of bright colors: little children wearing pink and yellow, red and peach.

6. The Meis would come out of their cave every few days and **forage** for food supplies left on the road, and sometimes they would see something that they both agreed was a tragedy to leave behind.

Part II: Determining the Meaning -- Match the vocabulary words to their dictionary definitions.

___ 1. prospect   A. dull
___ 2. scheming   B. bringing back to life
___ 3. reviving   C. something expected
___ 4. engulfed   D. make a thorough search for
___ 5. drab   E. surrounded by something almost to the point of being lost in it
___ 6. forage   F. plotting to achieve an evil or illegal end

ANSWER KEY: VOCABULARY - *The Joy Luck Club*

The Joy Luck Club	Scar	The Red Candle	The Moon Lady
1. C	1. H	1. H	1. F
2. H	2. B	2. E	2. E
3. A	3. F	3. A	3. D
4. G	4. A	4. G	4. A
5. E	5. G	5. C	5. C
6. B	6. D	6. B	6. H
7. F	7. I	7. I	7. B
8. D	8. E	8. F	8. I
	9. C	9. D	9. G

Rules of the Game	Voice from the Wall	Half and Half	Two Kinds
1. G	1. B	1. H	1. C
2. F	2. F	2. F	2. E
3. D	3. A	3. G	3. A
4. E	4. E	4. D	4. B
5. A	5. H	5. A	5. F
6. I	6. C	6. B	6. D
7. C	7. D	7. C	
8. B	8. G	8. E	
9. H			

Rice Husband	Four Directions	Without Wood	Best Quality
1. B	1. C	1. F	1. B
2. D	2. F	2. D	2. E
3. A	3. B	3. G	3. G
4. F	4. E	4. C	4. A
5. E	5. A	5. A	5. D
6. C	6. D	6. B	6. C
	7. G	7. E	7. F

Magpies	Waiting Between the Trees	Double Face	A Pair of Tickets
1. G	1. D	1. E	1. C
2. D	2. G	2. F	2. F
3. A	3. B	3. A	3. B
4. E	4. A	4. C	4. E
5. F	5. E	5. B	5. A
6. B	6. C	6. D	6. D
7. C	7. F		

DAILY LESSONS

LESSON ONE

Objective
To introduce **The Joy Luck Club** unit by giving students background information about China

Activity
One good way to introduce this unit is to have someone who is of Chinese heritage or someone who has visited China come and talk with your class about their own personal experiences. Photos, souvenirs, slides, videos, etc. would certainly add interest to the presentation.

If no one who has been to China is available, then check with a local travel agency to see if anyone there knows enough about China to make a presentation to your class. Any brochures, travel films, maps or other visual aids would be good additions to the agent's presentation.

It would probably be helpful to the presenter to have some information ahead of time about The Joy Luck Club. You might try pulling just a few incidents out of the book for the presenter.

Finally, if there is no one who can give a "live" presentation to your class, check out one of many different available videos about China. Look for ones that have information about Chinese history and culture as well as information about China today.

Have the presentation or show the film. Allow ample time for students' questions and some discussion. If you have a presenter, it might be nice to also serve Chinese tea and perhaps some fortune cookies if these kinds of activities are allowed in your school. If you have a presenter, be sure to have your students write a thank-you note to the presenter.

LESSON TWO

Objectives
1. To distribute the books and other materials students will need for this unit
2. To preview the study questions, do the vocabulary worksheets and read Reading Assignments 1 and 2

Activity #1
Distribute the materials students will use in this unit. Explain in detail how students are to use these materials.

Study Guides Students should preview the study guide questions before each reading assignment to get a feeling for important events and ideas in that section. After reading the section, students will (as a class or individually) answer the questions to review the events and ideas from that section of the book. Students should keep the study guides as study materials for the unit test.

Joy Luck Club - Daily Lessons - page 2

Vocabulary   Prior to reading a reading assignment, students will do vocabulary work related to the section of the book they are about to read. You might alert students to watch for the vocabulary words and note the sentences in which the words appear. This will help them to complete the vocabulary work more easily. After the book is read, there will be a vocabulary review of all the words used in the vocabulary assignments. Students should keep their vocabulary work as study materials for the unit test.

Reading Assignment Sheet   You need to fill in the reading assignment sheet to let students know when their reading has to be completed. You can either write the assignment sheet on a side blackboard or bulletin board and leave it there for students to see each day, or you can "ditto" copies for each student to have. In either case, you should advise students to become very familiar with the reading assignments so they know what is expected of them.

Extra Activities Center   The Unit Resource portion of this unit contains suggestions for a classroom library of related books and articles as well as crossword and word search puzzles. Make an extra activities center in your room where you keep these materials for student use. (Bring the books and articles from the library and keep several copies of the puzzles on hand.) Explain to students that these materials are available for them to use when they finish reading assignments or other class work early.

Nonfiction Assignment Sheet   Explain to students that they each are to read at least one nonfiction piece at some time during the unit. Students will fill out a nonfiction assignment sheet after completing the reading to help you evaluate their reading experiences and to help the students think about and evaluate their own reading experiences.

Activity #2
Show students how to preview the study questions and do the vocabulary worksheets for the first story, *The Joy Luck Club*. Perhaps it would be a good idea to do the first set together as a class. Making an overhead transparency of the first worksheet and using the overhead projector to fill in the answers as the class does the worksheet might be helpful for students.

Activity #3
Have students read the first story, *The Joy Luck Club*, out loud in class. Choose the best way to get readers within your class; pick students at random, ask for volunteers, or use whatever method works best for your group. If you have not yet completed an oral reading evaluation for your students this marking period, this would be a good opportunity to do so. A form is included with this unit for your convenience.

Students should finish the first story and also the previewing, vocabulary and reading work for *Scar* prior to your next class meeting.

NONFICTION ASSIGNMENT SHEET - *The Joy Luck Club*
(To be completed after reading the required nonfiction article)

Name _____ Date _____

Title of Nonfiction Read _____

Written By _____ Publication Date _____

I. Factual Summary: Write a short summary of the piece you read.

II. Vocabulary
    1. With which vocabulary words in the piece did you encounter some degree of difficulty?

    2. How did you resolve your lack of understanding with these words?

III. Interpretation: What was the main point the author wanted you to get from reading his work?

IV. Criticism
    1. With which points of the piece did you agree or find easy to accept? Why?

    2. With which points of the piece did you disagree or find difficult to believe? Why?

V. Personal Response: What do you think about this piece? OR How does this piece influence your ideas?

ORAL READING EVALUATION - *The Joy Luck Club*

Name _____ Class____ Date _____

SKILL	EXCELLENT	GOOD	AVERAGE	FAIR	POOR
Fluency	5	4	3	2	1
Clarity	5	4	3	2	1
Audibility	5	4	3	2	1
Pronunciation	5	4	3	2	1
_____	5	4	3	2	1
_____	5	4	3	2	1

Total _____   Grade _____

Comments:

LESSON THREE

Objectives
1. To review the main ideas and events from reading assignments 1 & 2
2. To preview and read reading assignment 3

Activity #1
Discuss the answers to the study questions for the first reading assignment in detail. Write the answers on the board or overhead transparency so students can have the correct answers for study purposes. Note: It is a good practice in public speaking and leadership skills for individual students to take charge of leading the discussions of the study questions. Perhaps a different student could go to the front of the class and lead the discussion each day that the study questions are discussed during this unit. Of course, the teacher should guide the discussion when appropriate and be sure to fill in any gaps the students leave.

Activity #2
Have students do the pre-reading, vocabulary and reading work for reading assignment 3 during this class period. This assignment should be completed prior to your next class meeting.

LESSON FOUR

Objectives
1. To review the main ideas and events of reading assignment 3
2. To give students the opportunity to practice their writing skills
3. To give students the opportunity to express their personal opinions
4. To have students think once more about each of the four stories they have read so far
5. To have students preview and read reading assignment #4

Activity #1
Distribute Writing Assignment #1. Discuss the directions in detail and give students this class period to complete this assignment.

Follow - Up: After you have graded the assignments, have a writing conference with the students. (This unit schedules one in Lesson 8.) After the writing conference, allow students to revise their papers using your suggestions and corrections. Give them about three days from the date they receive their papers to complete the revision. Grading the revisions on an A-C-E scale (all revisions well-done, some revisions made, few or no revisions made) works well for these evaluations. This will speed your grading time and still give some credit for the students' efforts.

Activity #2
Students should complete the previewing, vocabulary and reading work for reading assignment #4 prior to your next class meeting. Students who finish writing early should begin working on this assignment.

WRITING ASSIGNMENT #1 - *The Joy Luck Club*

PROMPT
The Joy Luck Club is essentially the story of four mothers and four daughters and their lives and relationships. Your assignment is to stop and think about your relationship with your own mother, stepmother, grandmother or other motherly-type person in your life and to write a composition in which you describe your relationship with that person.

PREWRITING
Think about this person and your relationship with her. Write down three words that describe your relationship. Under each word, give several examples of ways it is shown in your relationship. For example, if you say your relationship with this person is "close," you should tell some things you do together that show your close relationship - every Saturday you go shopping together; you share your personal thoughts with her, you try to do extra things for her to help out. The idea is to give specific examples for each word you choose.

DRAFTING
Write an introductory paragraph telling who the person is you are writing about. Tell a little about her and lead up to stating a sentence describing your relationship with that person, including all three of the descriptive words you chose in the pre-writing section above.

In the body of your composition, write one paragraph about each of the three words you chose. Within each paragraph, give the specific examples of things that show or exemplify that quality or description.

Write a concluding paragraph with your final thoughts or wishes for the future regarding your relationship with your person.

PEER CONFERENCE/REVISING
When you finish the rough draft of your paper, ask a student who sits near you to read it. After reading your rough draft, he/she should tell you what he/she liked best about your work, which parts were difficult to understand, and ways in which your work could be improved. Reread your paper considering your critic's comments, and make the corrections you think are necessary.

PROOFREADING
Do a final proofreading of your paper double-checking your grammar, spelling, organization, and the clarity of your ideas.

LESSON FIVE

Objectives
1. To review the main ideas and events from reading assignment 4
2. To preview and read reading assignment 5

Activity #1
Discuss the study questions to reading assignment 4 as you have done with the other study questions. If you wish, you could use the multiple choice questions as a quiz for reading assignment 4.

Activity #2
Give students this class period to complete the pre-reading and vocabulary work and to read assignment 5 silently in class. Tell students that this assignment should be completed prior to the next class period. If you have not yet completed the oral reading evaluations, you could have students read orally so you could complete the evaluations.

LESSON SIX

Objectives
1. To review the main ideas and events from reading assignment 5
2. To preview and read reading assignment 6

Activity #1
Discuss the study questions to reading assignment 5 as you have done with the other study questions. If you wish, you could use the multiple choice questions as a quiz for reading assignment 5.

Activity #2
Give students this class period to complete the pre-reading and vocabulary work and to read assignment 6 silently in class. Tell students that this assignment should be completed prior to the next class period. If you have not yet completed the oral reading evaluations, you could have students read orally so you could complete the evaluations.

LESSON SEVEN

Objectives
1. To review the main ideas and events in reading assignment 6
2. To give students the opportunity to do the required research for the nonfiction reading assignment

Activity #1
Discuss the answers to the study questions for assignment 6. Use the multiple choice question sheets as a quiz if you wish.

Activity #2
Take the students to the library. Remind them that one of their assignments with this unit is to read at least one article of nonfiction that is in some way related to the book *The Joy Luck Club*. It can be something about China (history, customs, places - anything), something about chess or Chinese food or Chinatown - the topic only has to relate in some way to the book. Students should be able to find something that interests them. As long as they can explain how it relates to the book, the article would be acceptable.

Activity #3
Students should fill out their Nonfiction Assignment Sheets after they read their articles.

LESSON EIGHT

Objectives
1. To give students the opportunity to practice writing to inform
2. To give students the opportunity to practice writing from their notes
3. To preview and read assignment 7

Activity #1
Distribute Writing Assignment #2. Discuss the directions in detail and give students this class period to write their compositions.

Activity #2
While students are working on their writing assignments, use the time to have individual conferences with students about their first writing assignment and to answer any questions they may have about doing their second writing assignment. A Writing Evaluation Form is included in this unit for your convenience.

Activity #3
Tell students that prior to the next class period they should have done the pre-reading, vocabulary and reading work for assignment 7. Suggest that students try to isolate some particular scenes that they can envision in the story. Ask them to pretend that they are seeing these scenes on television or in a movie. Tell them to think about the scenes (how the people in them would look, exactly what lines they would speak, how they would gesture, etc.) and to bring ideas about them to class.

WRITING ASSIGNMENT #2 - *The Joy Luck Club*

PROMPT
Waverly played chess. The members of the Joy Luck Club played mahjong. Think about a game you like to play. You could be writing about a card game, a board game, an outdoors game, a computer game, etc. Your assignment is to write a composition describing how to do or play the game that you most enjoy.

PREWRITING
First, think of all the things you like to do. What game or activity do you like best? Maybe it's a sports activity - or perhaps it is a kind of craft or other activity. Choose the thing you most enjoy playing.

Jot down some reasons why you like to play the game. Then, think about exactly what you have to do to PLAY it. Are there any special things needed to play it? Write down what they are. Jot down some notes about what it is and how it is done. Place them in a logical order - perhaps a chronological order (in order of time), or in a sequence of steps that need to be done.

DRAFTING
Write a paragraph in which you introduce your topic. You could start by telling when you play this game, and what you think of it.

In the body of your composition, describe exactly what the game is and exactly how it is done. This may take one paragraph, or it may take several paragraphs, depending on the game.

Write a concluding paragraph in which you wrap up your ideas.

PEER CONFERENCE/REVISING
When you finish your rough draft, ask a student who sits near you to read it. After reading your rough draft, he/she should tell you what he/she liked best about your work, which parts were difficult to understand, and ways in which your work could be improved. Reread your paper considering your critic's comments and make the corrections you think are necessary.

PROOFREADING
Do a final proofreading of your paper double-checking your grammar, spelling, organization, and the clarity of your ideas.

WRITING EVALUATION FORM - *The Joy Luck Club*

Name _____ Date _____

Writing Assignment #___ for the **The Joy Luck Club** unit Grade _____

Circle One For Each Item:

Description (paragraph 1)	excellent	good	fair	poor
Plans (body paragraphs)	excellent	workable	fair	not realistic
Conclusion	excellent	good	fair	poor
Grammar:	excellent	good	fair	poor (errors noted)
Spelling:	excellent	good	fair	poor (errors noted)
Punctuation:	excellent	good	fair	poor (errors noted)
Legibility:	excellent	good	fair	poor

Strengths:

Weaknesses:

Comments/Suggestions:

LESSON NINE

Objectives
1. To show students another way of visualizing their reading
2. To work with the book through role playing (You will continue to use the study questions and vocabulary words as usual, but this class period will give you and your students the opportunity to do something different with the story)
3. To encourage students to read parts of a book more closely
4. To review the main ideas and events from reading assignment 7
5. To do the pre-reading and reading work for reading assignment 8

Activity #1
Discuss the study questions for reading assignment 7. Use the multiple choice questions as a quiz if you choose to do so.

Activity #2
Have students volunteer to role play using various scenes within the story *Rice Husband*. For example, have Lena speaking with her mother when the mother tells her about one of the "bad" things that she has envisioned. Have three students play Mr. and Mrs. St. Clair and Lena on the morning when the death of Arnold Reisman is announced. Have two students pretend to be Lena and Harold discussing how to pay some bills. Whatever scenarios students find interesting will be fine.

Through this activity, students may learn to look a little more closely at the nuance of a story and to think more deeply about the people in the stories and their motivations.

Activity #3
Give students this class period to preview the study questions, do the vocabulary worksheet and read assignment 8. Students may read silently.

LESSON TEN

Objectives
1. To review the main ideas and events from reading assignment 8
2. To do the pre-reading and reading work for reading assignment 9

Activity #1
Discuss the study questions for reading assignment 8. Use the multiple choice questions as a quiz if you choose to do so.

Activity #2
Give students this class period to preview the study questions, do the vocabulary worksheet and read assignment 9. Students may read silently.

LESSON ELEVEN

Objectives
1. To review the main ideas and events from reading assignment 9
2. To introduce students to the game of chess

Activity #1
Discuss the study questions for reading assignment 9. Again, use the quiz for this story if necessary.

Activity #2
On the pages that follow are the templates for creating a chess game for your students to use. You should copy enough playing boards so that there is one board for every two students in your class. Likewise, there should be a set of playing pieces to go with each board. If there is a chess club at your school, perhaps you could get some of its members to demonstrate the game and to explain its rules. A rule sheet is included in this unit as well. Demonstrate to students how the game is played and explain the rules thoroughly.

You might want to see how many students in your class already know how to play chess, and pair up students who do know how to play with students who have never played the game before.

Give students a chance to experiment with playing the game. Chess is a game of skill and logic and is an excellent game for developing the mind. It is a good thing to encourage.

LESSON TWELVE

Objective
To preview and read assignment 10

Activity
Tell students that prior to the next class period they should have done the previewing, vocabulary and reading work for assignment 10. Give students this class period to work on this assignment. You could do some of the previewing and vocabulary work together as a class if you choose. Perhaps you could make a transparency of the vocabulary worksheet for this story and do it together as a class.

Use this as a template for the chess boards. You may want to enlarge it if your school's copier has that capability.

ROOK	KNIGHT	BISHOP	KING	QUEEN	BISHOP	KNIGHT	ROOK
PAWN	PAWN	PAWN	PAWN	PAWN	PAWN	PAWN	PAWN
PAWN	PAWN	PAWN	PAWN	PAWN	PAWN	PAWN	PAWN
ROOK	KNIGHT	BISHOP	QUEEN	KING	BISHOP	KNIGHT	ROOK

Use this as a template for the chess game pieces. They can be copied and cut out.

LESSON THIRTEEN

Objectives
1. To review the main ideas and events of reading assignment 10
2. To preview and read assignment 11

Activity #1
Discuss the study questions for assignment 10. Use the multiple choice questions if you need a quiz.

Activity #2
Give students this class period to do the pre-reading, vocabulary and reading work for assignment 12. This assignment should be completed prior to the next class meeting.

LESSON FOURTEEN

Objectives
1. To review the main ideas and events of reading assignment 11
2. To share nonfiction information from students' research
3. To increase students' breadth of knowledge about a variety of topics
4. To preview and read assignment 12

Activity #1
Discuss the study questions for reading assignment 11. Use the multiple choice version as a quiz if necessary.

Activity #2
Make sure students have their Nonfiction Assignment Sheets out and give them a few minutes to review their notes. Call on students to tell about the nonfiction articles they read. Have all students take a turn so that the entire group can hear about a variety of topics. Discuss any topics that are of particular interest to you or the class or ones that relate especially well to the book.

Activity #3
Tell students that prior to the next class period they should complete the previewing, vocabulary and reading work for reading assignment 12

As they do the reading assignment for *Double Face*, students should think about the story's two main characters, Lindo and Waverly Jong. By this point in the book, students know a good deal about these two women. Students might want to refer back to *The Red Candle*, *Rules of the Game*, and *Four Directions* for reminders about details about the characters. Tell them that the next lesson in class will be to discuss Lindo and Waverly Jong and to tell which character they think is most sympathetic, funniest, angriest, most confused, most caring-you can fill in whatever descriptive phrases you choose.

LESSON FIFTEEN

Objectives
1. To review the main ideas and events of reading assignment 12
2. To complete the pre-reading and reading work for assignment 13
3. To encourage students to draw on all of their knowledge of characters in stories
4. To teach students to examine characters as they develop over the course of several stories
5. To give students the opportunity to express their personal views about characters in class

Activity #1
Discuss the study questions for reading assignment 12. Use the multiple choice questions as a quiz if you need to check students' work.

Activity #2
Break students into small groups. Have them make group lists of all of Lindo and Waverly's strengths and weaknesses, listing no more than five strengths and five weaknesses for each. Then ask them to apply the list of descriptive terms that you have decided upon. Limit the terms you use to no more than two or three. Students should be ready to demonstrate these traits in each woman over the course of the stories they have read to date.

Bring the groups back into a whole-class setting. Ask students to quickly choose one person to report for them. Allow each group's reporter to tell the strengths and weaknesses of both women and, if time permits, to show where in the stories they believe each woman demonstrates the traits that you have chosen. Try to allow for differences among the groups and some good-natured disagreement.

Activity #3
Students should do the pre-reading, vocabulary and reading work for reading assignment 13. Choose whether you wish to have your students read silently or orally. This assignment should be completed prior to the next class period.

LESSON SIXTEEN

Objectives
1. To review the main events of reading assignment 13
2. To give students the opportunity to practice writing to persuade

Activity #1
Discuss the study questions for reading assignment 13

Activity #2
Distribute Writing Assignment #3. Discuss the directions in detail. Give students ample time to complete the assignment.

WRITING ASSIGNMENT #3 - *The Joy Luck Club*

PROMPT
For this assignment, you are to pretend to be one of the "aunties" and write in her voice to one of the daughters (not her own) to persuade the daughter to be more tolerant and appreciative of her mother.

PREWRITING
Think about the aunties and their daughters. Which characters did you enjoy the most? Which daughter was the most intolerant or unappreciative? Which of her aunties do you think could best approach her about being more tolerant and appreciative? Choose an auntie and a daughter to use in your composition.

Under the auntie's name, write down several of her main characteristics. Under the daughter's name, write down several ways she is intolerant or unappreciative. Finally, under the mother's name write down things she has done or reasons why she deserves more tolerance or appreciation.

Write down three reasons why the daughter should be more appreciative or tolerant of her mother. Under each reason, give at least one example of the point you are making.

As you write, you must remember the personalities of each of the people involved - the auntie (so you can write as she would have written), the daughter (so you know the best way to approach her), and the mother (so that you know why she deserves more tolerance or appreciation).

DRAFTING
Write your composition as a friendly letter. In your first paragraph, find a way to bring up the subject of the daughter's intolerance for her mother, to introduce the main idea of the letter.

In the body of the letter write one paragraph for each reason the auntie gives. Within each paragraph, give specific examples to show the main point.

Write a concluding paragraph in which you perhaps express your desire for the daughter to at least consider being a little more tolerant or a little more appreciative of her mother.

PEER CONFERENCE/REVISING
When you finish your rough draft, ask a student who sits near you to read it. After reading your rough draft, he/she should tell you what he/she liked best about your work, which parts were difficult to understand, and ways in which your work could be improved. Reread your paper considering your critic's comments and make the corrections you think are necessary.

PROOFREADING
Do a final proofreading of your paper double-checking your grammar, spelling, organization, and the clarity of your ideas.

LESSON SEVENTEEN

Objective
To review all of the vocabulary work done in this unit

Activity
   Choose one (or more) of the vocabulary review activities listed below and spend your class period as directed in the activity. Some of the materials for these review activities are located in the Vocabulary Resources section of this unit.

VOCABULARY REVIEW ACTIVITIES

1. Divide your class into two teams and have an old-fashioned spelling or definition bee.
2. Give each of your students (or students in groups of two, three or four) a *Joy Luck Club* Vocabulary Word Search Puzzle. The person (group) to find all of the vocabulary words in the puzzle first wins.
3. Give students a **Joy Luck Club** Vocabulary Word Search Puzzle without the word list. The person or group to find the most vocabulary words in the puzzle wins.
4. Use a **Joy Luck Club** Vocabulary Crossword Puzzle. Put the puzzle onto a transparency on the overhead projector (so everyone can see it), and do the puzzle together as a class.
5. Give students a **Joy Luck Club** Vocabulary Matching Worksheet to do.
6. Divide your class into two teams. Use the **Joy Luck Club** vocabulary words with their letters jumbled as a word list. Student 1 from Team A faces off against Student 1 from Team B. You write the first jumbled word on the board. The first student (1A or 1B) to unscramble the word wins the chance for his/her team to score points. If 1A wins the jumble, go to student 2A and give him/her a definition. He/she must give you the correct spelling of the vocabulary word which fits that definition. If he/she does, Team A scores a point, and you give student 3A a definition for which you expect a correctly spelled matching vocabulary word. Continue giving Team A definitions until some team member makes an incorrect response. An incorrect response sends the game back to the jumbled-word face off, this time with students 2A and 2B. Instead of repeating giving definitions to the first few students of each team, continue with the student after the one who gave the last incorrect response on the team. For example, if Team B wins the jumbled-word face-off, and student 5B gave the last incorrect answer for Team B, you would start this round of definition questions with student 6B, and so on. The team with the most points wins!
7. Have students write a story in which they correctly use as many vocabulary words as possible. Have students read their compositions orally! Post the most original compositions on your bulletin board!

LESSONS EIGHTEEN AND NINETEEN

Objectives
1. To discuss the ideas and themes from **The Joy Luck Club** in greater detail
2. To have students exercise their critical thinking skills
3. To try to relate some of the ideas in **The Joy Luck Club** to the students' lives

Activity #1
Choose the questions from the Extra Discussion Questions/Writing Assignments which seem most appropriate for your students. A class discussion of these questions is most effective if students have been given the opportunity to formulate answers to the questions prior to the discussion. To this end, you may either have all the students formulate answers to all the questions, divide your class into groups and assign one or more questions to each group, or you could assign one question to each student in your class. The option you choose will make a difference in the amount of class time needed for this activity.

Activity #2
After students have had ample time to formulate answers to the questions, begin your class discussion of the questions and the ideas presented by the questions. Be sure students take notes during the discussion so they have information to study for the unit test.

EXTRA DISCUSSION QUESTIONS/WRITING ASSIGNMENTS
The Joy Luck Club

Interpretive
1. How is point of view used in the book, and what effect does using it this way have?
2. Discuss the use of setting in the book.
3. Are the characters in **The Joy Luck Club** stereotypes? If so, explain the usefulness of employing stereotypes in the book. If they are not, explain how they merit individuality.
4. What are the main conflicts in the story? Are they resolved? If so, how? If not, why not?
5. Amy Tan uses the words "and" and "but" often to start sentences. What is the effect of this stylistic device?
6. Compare and contrast the four daughters.
7. Compare and contrast the four mothers.
8. Compare and contrast any of the minor characters that you find particularly interesting, including the fathers.
9. Compare and contrast the relationships of the daughters with the mothers.

Critical
10. Explain the significance of the title **The Joy Luck Club.**
11. Explain the significance of the titles of the stories of the book and why the stories that are included in each section fit there.
12. Explain the significance of each of the titles of the stories.
13. Discuss the structure of the book. In what order are the stories told? Why do you think they are told that way?
14. Make a list of the most important secondary characters in the book and explain how each is important.
15. Describe Amy Tan's writing style. How does it influence our perception of the story?
16. Who is the main character of the book? Defend your choice.
17. What themes are present in **The Joy Luck Club**? Explain each.
18. What is one of the main points of the book **The Joy Luck Club**? Explain with details from the text.

Critical/Personal Response
19. The book is set up so that you sometimes read about one person from another person's point of view. Then you read about the person from their own point of view. For example, in *Rules of the Game*, you read about Lindo Jong from her daughter's viewpoint. Later, though, in *Double Face,* you get to see Lindo's point of view about herself and about her daughter. Some shifts in point of view are bound to change our minds sometimes when we read a second, or perhaps a third, story. Demonstrate one example of how this happened to you as you progressed through **The Joy Luck Club.**
20. The original name of **The Joy Luck Club** was **Wind and Water**. Which title do you think is best? Why?
21. Which of the mothers and which of the daughters do you think is most interesting? Why?
22. According to Amy Tan's stories, what kind of relationship do most mothers and daughters have?
23. If you had to choose one of the mothers to be *your* mother, which one would you choose? Why?
24. If you were a parent to one of the daughters, which one would you want to be your child? Why?

Personal Response
25. Which story was your personal favorite? Why?
26. Choose one story you think could be expanded into a full-length novel. Give some examples of how it could be expanded.
27. Do you think the mothers and daughters in the stories are typical of mothers and daughters in general?
28. Of all the minor characters (not mothers or daughters) in **The Joy Luck Club**, which is your favorite and why? (You may also alter this question or questions #'s 29, 30, or 31 and tell which is your *least* favorite.)
29. Of all the mothers in **The Joy Luck Club,** which is your favorite and why?
30. Of all the daughters in **The Joy Luck Club,** which is your favorite and why?
31. Of all the men in **The Joy Luck Club**, which is your favorite and why?

LESSON TWENTY

Objective

To review the main ideas presented in **The Joy Luck Club**

Activity #1

Choose one of the review games/activities included in the packet and spend your class period as outlined there. Some materials for these activities are located in the Extra Activities Packet section of this unit.

Activity #2

Remind students that the Unit Test will be in the next class meeting. Stress the review of the Study Guides and their class notes as a last-minute, brush-up review for homework. Invite questions if students still have any.

REVIEW GAMES/ACTIVITIES - *The Joy Luck Club*

1. Ask the class to make up a unit test for **The Joy Luck Club**. The test should have 4 sections: matching, true/false, short answer, and essay. Students may use 1/2 period to make the test and then swap papers and use the other 1/2 class period to take a test a classmate has devised (open book). You may want to use the unit test included in this packet or take questions from the students' unit tests to formulate your own test.

2. Take 1/2 period for students to make up true and false questions (including the answers). Collect the papers and divide the class into two teams. Draw a big tic-tac-toe board on the chalk board. Make one team X and one team O. Ask questions to each side, giving each student one turn. If the question is answered correctly, that students' team's letter (X or O) is placed in the box. If the answer is incorrect, no mark is placed in the box. The object is to get three marks in a row like tic-tac-toe. You may want to keep track of the number of games won for each team.

3. Take 1/2 period for students to make up questions (true/false and short answer). Collect the questions. Divide the class into two teams. You'll alternate asking questions to individual members of teams A & B (like in a spelling bee). The question keeps going from A to B until it is correctly answered, then a new question is asked. A correct answer does not allow the team to get another question. Correct answers are +2 points; incorrect answers are -1 point.

4. Have students pair up and quiz each other from their study guides and class notes.

5. Give students a **The Joy Luck Club** crossword puzzle to complete.

6. Divide your class into two teams. Use the **Joy Luck Club** crossword words with their letters jumbled as a word list. Student 1 from Team A faces off against Student 1 from Team B. You write the first jumbled word on the board. The first student (1A or 1B) to unscramble the word wins the chance for his/her team to score points. If 1A wins the jumble, go to student 2A and give him/her a clue. He/she must give you the correct word which matches that clue. If he/she does, Team A scores a point, and you give student 3A a clue for which you expect another correct response. Continue giving Team A clues until some team member makes an incorrect response. An incorrect response sends the game back to the jumbled-word face off, this time with students 2A and 2B. Instead of repeating giving clues to the first few students of each team, continue with the student after the one who gave the last incorrect response on the team. For example, if Team B wins the jumbled-word face-off, and student 5B gave the last incorrect answer for Team B, you would start this round of clue questions with student 6B, and so on.

UNIT TESTS

SHORT ANSWER UNIT TEST #1 - *The Joy Luck Club*

I. Matching/Identify

___ 1. Waverly   A. Lena's husband

___ 2. Tyan-yu   B. He owned the house where An-mei and her mother lived

___ 3. Chong   C. Ying-ying's daughter

___ 4. Wu Tsing   D. Lindo Jong's daughter

___ 5. Harold   E. Piano teacher

___ 6. Suyuan   F. Rose's husband

___ 7. Ted   G. Jing-mei's mother

___ 8. Lena   H. Lindo's husband via the matchmaker

II. Short Answer

1. Why did Jing-mei's mother form the Joy Luck Club in Kweilin?

2. Why did the women in Kweilin call the club Joy Luck?

3. What was the "art of invisible strength" that Waverly Jong's mother taught her?

4. Why did Waverly run away from her mother when they were shopping?

5. What was in Rose's mother's little Chinese book, **The Twenty-Six Malignant Gates**?

Joy Luck Club - Unit Test 1 - page2

6. What did Jing-mei's mother lose in China?

7. What did Jing-mei realize after she had played both "Pleading Child" and "Perfectly Contented" a few times?

8. What was unusual about Lena and Harold's marriage?

9. When Rose was a child, what did her mother tell her about what she and mirrors could see?

10. According to Lindo, what would be the best combination in her children?

11. Why did Jing-mei's mother actually leave her babies in China?

12. "My sisters and I stand, arms around each other, laughing and wiping the tears from each other's eyes. The flash of the Polaroid goes off and my father hands me the snapshot. My sisters and I watch quietly together, eager to see what develops. The gray-green surface changes to the bright colors of our three images, sharpening and deepening all at once. And although we don't speak, I know we all see it: Together we look like our mother. Her same eyes, her same mouth, open in surprise to see, at last, her long-cherished wish." Who are "my sisters and I," and what is the long-cherished wish?

Joy Luck Club - Unit Test 1 - page 3

III. Essay

If you had to choose one person as the main character of the book, which character would it be? Justify your answer.

IV. Vocabulary

Listen to the vocabulary word and spell it. After you have spelled all the words, go back and write down the definitions.

1.

2.

3.

4.

5.

6.

7.

8.

9.

10.

SHORT ANSWER UNIT TEST #2 - *The Joy Luck Club*

I. Matching/Identify

___ 1. Waverly   A. Piano teacher

___ 2. Tyan-yu   B. Ying-ying's daughter

___ 3. Mr. Chong   C. Jing-mei's mother

___ 4. Wu Tsing   D. Lindo Jong's daughter

___ 5. Harold   E. Lena's husband

___ 6. Suyuan   F. Lindo's husband via the matchmaker

___ 7. Ted   G. He owned the house where An-mei and her mother lived

___ 8. Lena   H. Rose's husband

II. Short Answer

1. Why was Jing-mei invited to the Joy Luck Club?

2. What was the purpose of Lindo's tricking the Huangs?

3. Briefly describe the effect of Ying-ying's encounter with the Moon Lady.

4. Why did Waverly first stop playing chess?

5. What purpose does Bing's death serve in the story?

Joy Luck Club - Unit Test 2 - page 2

6. What is the significance of the poorly built table in *Rice Husband*?

7. In Waverly's relationship with her mother, why is it important that Lindo Jong is the "queen" while Waverly remains the "pawn"?

8. What are some examples of Rose Jordan's being "without wood," in her mother's words?

9. What kind of person is Waverly Jong based on the story, *Best Quality*?

10. What is An-mei's mother's final victory over Wu Tsing and why does she give up her life to achieve it?

11. In *Waiting Between the Trees*, what are some of the ways that the reader is led to believe from Ying-ying St. Clair that Lena St. Clair knows little about her mother?

12. Why is it ironic that in *Double Face* Waverly thinks that both she and her mother look "devious" and "two-faced"?

Joy Luck Club - Unit Test 2 - page 3

III. Essay
    What do we learn from **The Joy Luck Club**? Focus your answer on perhaps three things that we learn from the book. Explain your thoughts in detail using examples from the novel.

IV. Vocabulary
Listen to the vocabulary word and spell it. After you have spelled all the words, go back and write down the definitions.

1.

2.

3.

4.

5.

6.

7.

8.

9.

10

KEY: SHORT ANSWER UNIT TESTS - *The Joy Luck Club*

The short answer questions are taken directly from the study guides.
If you need to look up the answers, you will find them in the study guide section.

Answers to the composition questions will vary depending on your
class discussions and the level of your students.

For the vocabulary section of the test, choose ten of the
words from the vocabulary lists to read orally for your students.

The answers to the matching section of the test are below.

Answers to the matching section of the Advanced Short Answer Unit Test
are the same as for Short Answer Unit Test #2.

Test #1	Test #2
1. D	1. D
2. H	2. F
3. E	3. A
4. B	4. G
5. A	5. E
6. G	6. C
7. F	7. H
8. C	8. B

ADVANCED SHORT ANSWER UNIT TEST - *The Joy Luck Club*

I. Matching/Identify

___ 1. Waverly   A. Piano teacher

___ 2. Tyan-yu   B. Ying-ying's daughter

___ 3. Mr. Chong   C. Jing-mei's mother

___ 4. Wu Tsing   D. Lindo Jong's daughter

___ 5. Harold   E. Lena's husband

___ 6. Suyuan   F. Lindo's husband via the matchmaker

___ 7. Ted   G. He owned the house where An-mei and her mother lived

___ 8. Lena   H. Rose's husband

II. Short Answer

1. Discuss the structure of the book. In what order are the stories told? Why do you think they are told that way?

2. Explain the significance of the titles of the sections of the book and why the stories that are included in each section fit there.

3. Explain the significance of each of the titles of the stories.

Joy Luck Club - Advanced Short Answer Unit Test - page 2

4. Make a list of three of the most important secondary characters in the book and explain how each is important.

5. Who is the main character of the book? Defend your choice.

6. What themes are present in **The Joy Luck Club**? Explain each.

7. What is one of the main points of the book, **The Joy Luck Club**? Explain with details from the text.

Joy Luck Club - Advanced Short Answer Unit Test - page 3

III. Essay
Choose one mother-daughter conflict in **The Joy Luck Club**. Explain the conflict thoroughly and give at least three examples of how it is manifested in the stories.

IV. Vocabulary
Listen to the vocabulary words and write them down. After you have written down all of the words, write a paragraph in which you use all the words. The paragraph must in some way relate to **The Joy Luck Club**.

MULTIPLE CHOICE UNIT TEST #1- *The Joy Luck Club*

I. Matching

___ 1. Waverly   A. Lena's husband

___ 2. Tyan-yu   B. He owned the house where An-mei and her mother lived

___ 3. Chung   C. Ying-ying's daughter

___ 4. Wu Tsing   D. Lindo Jong's daughter

___ 5. Harold   E. Piano teacher

___ 6. Suyuan   F. Rose's husband

___ 7. Ted   G. Jing-mei's mother

___ 8. Lena   H. Lindo's husband via the matchmaker

II. Short Answer

1. Why did Jing-mei's mother form the Joy Luck Club in Kweilin?
   a. because she had nothing to do and craved entertainment
   b. because it was very fashionable in China to form clubs
   c. because it gave her and her friends a diversion from the horrors of the war
   d. because there were no good places to in Kweilin to eat

2. Why did the women in Kweilin call the club Joy Luck?
   a. They wanted to find something that sounded good translated into Chinese.
   b. They voted three times, and that name was the big winner.
   c. In Chinese, Joy Luck means "great food."
   d. The club was called Joy Luck because the women hoped to be lucky and that hope was their only joy.

3. What was the "art of invisible strength" that Waverly Jong's mother taught her?
   a. It was a way of building muscles without people knowing about it.
   b. It was a way of cheating at chess without getting caught.
   c. It was a special way of playing mahjong so that one always won.
   d. It was a strategy for winning arguments and respect from others.

Joy Luck Club - Multiple Choice Unit Test 1 - page 2

4. Why did Waverly run away from her mother when they were shopping?
    a. because her mother kept embarrassing her by showing off, and Waverly couldn't stand it any longer
    b. because she really disliked watching her mother shop for her little brothers
    c. because her mother told her that she really wasn't so good at playing chess
    d. because she saw an old boyfriend while they were in a clothing store

5. What was in Rose's mother's little Chinese book, **The Twenty-Six Malignant Gates**?
    a. The book contained many little stories of successful Chinese girls.
    b. The book contained the names of everyone Rose's mother thought was evil.
    c. The book told stories of many people who had tried to get into China illegally.
    d. The book showed children's predispositions to certain dangers on certain days, based on their Chinese birthdates.

6. What did Jing-mei's mother lose in China?
    a. her will to live
    b. her spirit
    c. her mother and father, her family home, her first husband, and her twin baby girls
    d. her mother's jade pendant

7. What did Jing-mei realize after she had played both "Pleading Child" and "Perfectly Contented" a few times?
    a. She realized that neither one was very well written musically.
    b. She realized that her mother had played them both years ago.
    c. She realized that they were two halves of the same song.
    d. She realized that she should have chosen to play "Perfectly Contented" instead of "Pleading Child" at her recital years ago.

8. What was unusual about Lena and Harold's marriage?
    a. They didn't live in the same house.
    b. They called each other by Chinese pet names.
    c. They tried to keep everything separate but equal.
    d. They voted on when to dine out and when to dine at home.

9. When Rose was a child, what did her mother tell her about what she and mirrors could see?
    a. She said that mirrors reflected her personality but that her mother formed it.
    b. She said that mirrors could see only Rose's face but that her mother could see her inside out even when Rose was not in the room.
    c. She said that mirrors lied but that she always told the truth.
    d. She said that mirrors could tell your fortune while your mother could only see what was on the outside in your face.

Joy Luck Club - Multiple Choice Unit Test 1 - page 3

10. According to Lindo, what would be the best combination in her children?
    a. Chinese looks and American manners
    b. American circumstances and Chinese character
    c. Chinese brains and American looks
    d. American height and Chinese thoughtfulness

11. Why did Jing-mei's mother actually leave her babies in China?
    a. She just didn't feel like carrying them anymore.
    b. She thought she was going to die and didn't want them to die with her.
    c. She wanted to kill them but didn't have the will to do so.
    d. She didn't want to bring them to America because they would spoil her chances of getting another husband.

12. "My sisters and I stand, arms around each other, laughing and wiping the tears from each other's eyes. The flash of the Polaroid goes off and my father hands me the snapshot. My sisters and I watch quietly together, eager to see what develops. The gray-green surface changes to the bright colors of our three images, sharpening and deepening all at once. And although we don't speak, I know we all see it: Together we look like our mother. Her same eyes, her same mouth, open in surprise to see, at last, her long-cherished wish."
    Who are "my sisters and I," and what is the long-cherished wish?
    a. "My sisters and I" are all of the women of China, and the long cherished wish is Jing-mei's long-held belief that she was destined to live out her days in China.
    b. "My sisters and I" are Jing-mei and her half-sisters, and the long-cherished wish is her mother's wish that the lost babies would be found and the family would be reunited.
    c. "My sisters and I" are all Chinese feminists, and the long-cherished wish was for a China where women were equal.
    d. "My sisters and I" are all of the aunties' children, and the long-cherished wish was that they would all get along with each other.

Joy Luck Club - Multiple Choice Unit Test 1 - page 4

III. Essay

Who is the most compassionate male figure in the book? Tell why you think so. Use details from the text.

Joy Luck Club - Multiple Choice Unit Test 1 - page 5

IV. Vocabulary   Match the vocabulary words to the definitions.

1. somber   A. foot doctor
2. cultivate   B. place of perfect happiness
3. concubines   C. wife or husband
4. invaded   D. agreement
5. illusion   E. dull
6. eluded   F. offensively self-satisfied smile
7. chasm   G. guard
8. sentinel   H. grow; encourage; promote
9. trivial   I. serious
10. mesmerizing   J. secondary wives
11. laments   K. of little importance
12. podiatrist   L. entrance hall
13. sonorous   M. false perception of reality
14. vulnerable   N. able to be hurt
15. foyer   O. hypnotizing
16. covenant   P. entered by force to conquer
17. nirvana   Q. escaped the understanding of
18. smirk   R. abyss; gorge; steep-sided hole
19. spouse   S. regrets
20. drab   T. full, deep or rich in sound

MULTIPLE CHOICE UNIT TEST #2 - *The Joy Luck Club*

I. Matching/Identify

___ 1. Waverly   A. Lindo's husband via the matchmaker

___ 2. Tyan-yu   B. Piano teacher

___ 3. Chung   C. Lindo Jong's daughter

___ 4. Wu Tsing   D. Jing-mei's mother

___ 5. Harold   E. Rose's husband

___ 6. Suyuan   F. He owned the house where An-mei and her mother lived

___ 7. Ted   G. Ying-ying's daughter

___ 8. Lena   H. Lena's husband

II. Short Answer

1. Why was Jing-mei invited to the Joy Luck Club?
    a. because no one else in the family knew how to play mahjong
    b. because her "aunties" wanted to tell her about her mother's lost babies and to give her money to go find them in China
    c. because her father wanted to attend and unaccompanied men weren't allowed
    d. because she is the one who suggested the name of the club in the first place

2. What was the purpose of Lindo's tricking the Huangs?
    a. It was her way of getting back at her parents.
    b. It was just a Chinese custom to see how long it would take to trick them.
    c. It was her way of getting free from her arranged marriage to Tyan-yu.
    d. It was a way of proving her worth to her daughter Waverly.

3. Briefly describe the effect of Ying-ying's encounter with the Moon Lady.
    a. The encounter made her laugh.
    b. The encounter was traumatic, filled her with despair, and she began to cry.
    c. The encounter was the high point of her whole boat ride that day.
    d. The encounter was left her feeling happy for weeks afterward.

Joy Luck Club - Multiple Choice Unit Test 2 - page 2

4. Why did Waverly first stop playing chess?
   a. because she never really liked it in the first place
   b. because she couldn't beat her brother, Vincent
   c. because she didn't have enough money to enter tournaments
   d. because she was angry with her mother's show-off attitude towards her playing

5. What purpose does Bing's death serve in the story?
   a. It demonstrates Rose and her mother's view of "faith."
   b. It demonstrates the difference between boys and girls.
   c. It shows how irresponsible Rose was when she was young.
   d. It shows how careless Chinese people are about their children.

6. What is the significance of the poorly built table in *Rice Husband*?
   a. It is a symbol of the fact that Lena's husband, Harold, has to use crutches.
   b. It is a symbol of the rift between Lena and her mother.
   c. It shows how Americans build things poorly while Chinese people build things well.
   d. It is significant because it was made poorly by Harold, but Lena pretends that it is fine.

7. In Waverly's relationship with her mother, why is it important that Lindo Jong is the "queen" while Waverly remains the "pawn"?
   a. because Waverly has never gotten over the time her mother beat her at chess
   b. because even though her mother isn't very talented, being the "queen" makes her seem important
   c. because Waverly hates any chess terms being used to describe her and her mother
   d. because Lindo can move from all directions and can always beat Waverly in real life

8. What are some examples of Rose Jordan's being "without wood," in her mother's words?
   a. She can't work out for very long, she has no will power, and she overeats all the time.
   b. She can't climb trees, used metal crutches when she broke her leg, and doesn't know anything about the vines in her garden.
   c. She listens to too many people, can't make up her own mind, and doesn't know what to tell Ted.
   d. She is foolish, watches too much television, and has no close friends.

Joy Luck Club - Multiple Choice Unit Test 2 - page 3

9. What kind of person is Waverly Jong based on the story, *Best Quality*?
    a. a disloyal person who flaunts what she has over others and walks crooked like a crab
    b. a fun person who is always great to invite to a party
    c. an insecure shrinking violet
    d. a very intelligent woman who always listens to her mother

10. What is An-mei's mother's final victory over Wu Tsing and why does she give up her life to achieve it?
    a. She gets Wu Tsing to take care of both of her children, and she gives up her life because she loves her children so much.
    b. She makes him feel bad, and she does it because she hates him so much.
    c. She makes him look bad, and she does it because she wants to teach him a lesson.
    d. She gets him to say he is sorry, and she does it because he was mean to her.

11. In *Waiting Between the Trees*, what are some of the ways that the reader is led to believe from Ying-ying St. Clair that Lena St. Clair knows little about her mother?
    a. Ying-ying says that Lena doesn't know that she was married before, that she aborted her first child, and that she is a tiger lady.
    b. Ying-ying says Lena doesn't know her age, her height, or her real hair color.
    c. Ying-ying says that Lena doesn't even know her real name, doesn't know where she was born, and doesn't know her first husband's name.
    d. Ying-ying says Lena doesn't know her real face, her real name, or her real nature.

12. Why is it ironic that in *Double Face* Waverly thinks that both she and her mother look "devious" and "two-faced"?
    a. because they actually look nothing whatever alike
    b. because Lindo isn't really Waverly's mother
    c. because Lindo has always prided herself on her honesty
    d. because Waverly has always wanted to be unlike her mother

III. Essay

What do we learn from **The Joy Luck Club**? Focus your answer on perhaps three things that we learn from the book. Explain your thoughts in detail using examples from the novel.

Joy Luck Club - Multiple Choice Unit Test 2 - page 5

IV. Vocabulary   Match the vocabulary words to their definitions.

1.	eluded	A.	foot doctor
2.	illusion	B.	place of perfect happiness
3.	chasm	C.	wife or husband
4.	invaded	D.	agreement
5.	cultivate	E.	dull
6.	somber	F.	offensively self-satisfied smile
7.	concubines	G.	guard
8.	sentinel	H.	grow; encourage; promote
9.	trivial	I.	serious
10.	mesmerizing	J.	secondary wives
11.	nirvana	K.	of little importance
12.	podiatrist	L.	entrance hall
13.	sonorous	M.	false perception of reality
14.	vulnerable	N.	able to be hurt
15.	foyer	O.	hypnotizing
16.	covenant	P.	entered by force to conquer
17.	laments	Q.	escaped the understanding of
18.	spouse	R.	abyss; gorge; steep-sided hole
19.	smirk	S.	regrets
20.	drab	T.	full, deep or rich in sound

ANSWER SHEET - *The Joy Luck Club*
Multiple Choice Unit Tests

I. Matching
1. ___
2. ___
3. ___
4. ___
5. ___
6. ___
7. ___
8. ___

II. Multiple Choice
1. ___
2. ___
3. ___
4. ___
5. ___
6. ___
7. ___
8. ___
9. ___
10. ___
11. ___
12. ___

IV. Vocabulary
1. ___
2. ___
3. ___
4. ___
5. ___
6. ___
7. ___
8. ___
9. ___
10. ___
11. ___
12. ___
13. ___
14. ___
15. ___
16. ___
17. ___
18. ___
19. ___
20. ___

ANSWER KEY - *The Joy Luck Club*
Multiple Choice Unit Tests

Answers to Unit Test 1 are in the left column. Answers to Unit Test 2 are in the right column.

I. Matching	II. Multiple Choice	IV. Vocabulary
1. D C	1. C B	1. I Q
2. H A	2. D C	2. H M
3. E B	3. D B	3. J R
4. B F	4. A D	4. P P
5. A H	5. D A	5. M H
6. G D	6. C D	6. Q I
7. F E	7. C D	7. R J
8. C G	8. C C	8. G G
	9. B A	9. K K
	10. B A	10. O O
	11. B A	11. S B
	12. B C	12. A A
		13. T T
		14. N N
		15. L L
		16. D D
		17. B S
		18. F C
		19. C F
		20. E E

UNIT RESOURCE MATERIALS

BULLETIN BOARD IDEAS - *The Joy Luck Club*

1. Save a space for students' best writing. Make a nice border. Cut out letters THE BEST or YOU'RE THE TOPS! with a cut-out top hat -- whatever title you want to show the meaning of the space. Staple up the best writing samples (or quizzes or whatever you have graded) on colorful paper.

2. Bring in (or have students bring in) pictures of mothers and daughters or mothers and sons from magazines. Make a collage if you have enough different pictures (or post individual pictures on colorful paper if you only have a few pictures). This could also be a fun introductory activity if students participate. You could have the border and title done for the bulletin board and invite students to staple up their own pictures wherever they want them. It will only take a few minutes of class time, but the students will enjoy it and you can get your bulletin board done in a hurry.

3. Draw one of the word search puzzles onto the bulletin board. (Be sure to enlarge it.) Write the key words to one side. Invite students to take their pens or markers and find the words before and/or after class (or perhaps this could be an activity for students who finish their work early).

4. Have students draw pictures of what they think a scene in **The Joy Luck Club** might look like. They could, for example, draw a picture of the place in Kweilin where Suyuan Woo left her twin daughters. Or they could draw a picture of the dinner table at the Chinese New Year's dinner when Suyuan had the crab with the missing leg. Post these drawings on the bulletin board.

5. Make a nice large clean space where single words and phrases can be posted. Have students cut words and phrases out of magazines, newspapers, and even advertisements. For example, they might find the word **MOTHER**, the words **RAPE**, **DISHONOR**, and **REVENGE**. They might find phrases such as **TWIN BABIES** or **FIRST HUSBAND** or **ACROSS THE BAY**. It doesn't really matter what the words and phrases are. The goal is to collect and post as many as possible that reflect people, themes, and events in **The Joy Luck Club**.

6. If you alert students early enough in the unit, they might be able to write to someone and acquire postage stamps from China. Maybe there could be a display of Chinese and American stamps on the bulletin board.

EXTRA ACTIVITIES - *The Joy Luck Club*

One of the difficulties in teaching a novel is that all students don't read at the same speed. One student who likes to read may take the book home and finish it in a day or two. Sometimes a few students finish the in-class assignments early. The problem, then, is finding suitable extra activities for students.

The best thing we've found is to keep a little library in the classroom. For this unit on **The Joy Luck Club,** you might check out from the school library other books by Tan. A biography of the author would be interesting for some students. You may include other related books and articles about mothers and daughters, Chinese customs, travel to China, ancient China, the attitudes toward female children in China in the past and today, etc.

Other things you may keep on hand are puzzles. We have made some relating directly to **The Joy Luck Club** for you. Feel free to duplicate them.

Some students may like to draw. You might devise a contest or allow some extra-credit grade for students who draw characters or scenes from **The Joy Luck Club.** Note, too, that if the students do not want to keep their drawings you may pick up some extra bulletin board materials this way. If you have a contest and you supply the prize (a popular CD or something like that perhaps), you could, possibly, make the drawing itself a non-refundable entry fee.

The pages which follow contain games, puzzles and worksheets. The keys, when appropriate, immediately follow the puzzle or worksheet. There are two main groups of activities: one group for the unit; that is, generally relating to **The Joy Luck Club** text, and another group of activities related strictly to **The Joy Luck Club** vocabulary.

Directions for the games, puzzles and worksheets are self-explanatory. The object here is to provide you with extra materials you may use in any way you choose.

MORE ACTIVITIES - *The Joy Luck Club*

1. Pick a chapter or scene with a great deal of dialogue and have the students act it out on a stage. (Perhaps you could assign various scenes to different groups of students so more than one scene could be acted and more students could participate.)

2. Show a film version of **The Joy Luck Club** to the class after you have completed reading the novel. Have students evaluate the movie and compare/contrast it with the book. If the students have tried writing a chapter into a scene in a play, you may wish to discuss how the problems they encountered in changing the form were handled in the movie.

3. Have students design a book cover (front and back and inside flaps) for **The Joy Luck Club.**

4. Have students design a bulletin board (ready to be put up; not just sketched) for **The Joy Luck Club.**

5. Have a guest speaker discuss travel to China today. Ask the person, perhaps a travel agent or someone who has traveled often to China for pleasure or business, to talk in depth about the places people like to visit, what exciting things there are to do, what things tourists should avoid, the attitude of the Chinese toward Americans, etc.

6. Use some of the related topics (noted earlier for an in-class library) as topics for research, reports or written papers, or as topics for guest speakers.

7. Ask students to think about which character in **The Joy Luck Club** they most identify with. Have students get up in front of the class and tell the class about themselves (in the role of the character they have chosen).

8. Have students hold a kind of mock trial. "Try" one of the mothers and one of the daughters for being uncooperative or unkind or just for being a poor mother or daughter. Then have another group of students play the lawyers and defend the person on trial from the "charges."

9. If you have students who are artistically talented, you might have them write a short musical piece, write a song, or choreograph a dance sequence based on one of the stories in **The Joy Luck Club**. The musical piece, song, or dance could then be performed for the whole class.

10. Have students pretend to be one of the characters in **The Joy Luck Club**. Have them write to the character that they most have problems with and explain those problems and possible solutions in writing.

WORD SEARCH - *The Joy Luck Club*

All the words in this list are associated with *The Joy Luck Club*. The words are placed backwards, forward, diagonally, up and down. The included words are listed below the word search.

```
O B R I G H T N E S S R E V O T F E L H
P P C H I N A U T C O U R G R T C L I N
O K I S N W N C R L U O Y E G I G D F B
P S W U N M L B X T P H E U R P G N E W
C K A W M A G N I R L S L B A U R A S B
O R V N I N R G E B U E O E Y N A C A W
L H E R F Z E T M N L T M N N B V H V S
D H R D Y R G B I C X E A N D A E I E D
N D L O N R A I E O Y Y O O O R L L R W
G U Y P F X B N M O T O O Z U C U D S F
C O Y G B O F G C K M W D G B R C T R W
C H U N G O U Y T I L A U Q L D K U I W
Y C O I U Z A R C E S V V Y E A Y O C T
Q R O N A I P T H S U C O T A T S H H Y
V N D V G H E A V E N J O K I N D S X W
```

ARNOLD	COOKIE	LENA	RICH	TIGER
ART	CRAB	LUCKY	RING	TREES
BIBLE	DOUBLE	MAN	RULES	TURTLE
BING	FOUND	MEIMEI	SHOU	TYANYU
BOAT	FOUR	MOLE	SHOUT	WAVERLY
BRIGHTNESS	GLASS	MOON	SOUP	WOOD
CANDLE	GRAVE	NINGPO	STCLAIR	WUSHI
CHANG	HEAVEN	OPIUM	SUN	SANFRANCISCO
CHILD	HSU	PIANO	SUYUAN	
CHINA	JOY	POPO	TAN	
CHOU	KINDS	QUALITY	TAO	
CHONG	LIFESAVERS	RED	TED	
COLD	LEFTOVERS	RICE		

CROSSWORD - *The Joy Luck Club*

CROSSWORD PUZZLE CLUES - *Joy Luck Club*

ACROSS

1. The women hoped to be __ and that was their only joy.
3. Waverly's family called her this
4. Having no respect for ancestors or family
6. Proof of the rotting marriage
8. Color of the candle
9. It was supposed to be lit at both ends and kept burning all night.
11. Lindo's husband via the matchmaker
14. ___ Face
15. Lindo taught Waverly the ___ of invisible strength
17. Ying-ying's wish was to be ___
19. ___ of the Game
20. Where An-mei's family lived in China
22. Lindo Jong's daughter
25. Waverly's neighbor who played chess with her
26. It burned An-mei the night her mother returned
29. Waverly's game
31. ___ Luck Club
32. Huang ___: Tyan-yu's mother
33. One with a lost leg on Chinese New Year is a bad sign
35. Ying-ying fell off the __ and got separated from her family
38. Ying-ying's daughter
39. Lena's mother's Chinese sign
41. Piano teacher
43. He drowned
45. If the lips are gone, the teeth will be ___.
47. Jong family hill: Three Steps to ___
48. On the third day after her mother died, An-mei learned to do this
49. Matchmaker suggested Lindo take off all her ___ to be better balanced
50. Two ___
51. Waiting Between the _____

DOWN

1. Meaning of 'yu' in Tyan-yu's name
2. Original setting for JLC meetings
3. Moon Lady became one
5. An-mei ___; Rose ___ Jordan
6. ____ Lady
7. Rose's sister
9. Necklace made of red jade
10. They took the place of the white knight and black pawn
11. Rose's husband
12. An-mei's personal maid; __ Chang
13. Moon Lady's husband ives there
16. This society gave Waverly her 2nd chess set
18. The Twenty-six Malignant _____
19. Rose's mother threw her blue sapphire one into the water
21. An-mei's name for her grandmother
22. Without ____
23. He actually got the chess set for Christmas
24. ___ Husband
27. Substance First Wife used
28. Instrument Jing-mei played
30. Jing-mei goes there to find her sisters
31. Jing-mei's American name
32. Lindo's village
34. Festival of Pure ___
35. Ying-ying got it on her clothes
36. ____ From the Wall
37. Rose defines it as an illusion that one is somehow in control.
38. Waverly's mother
39. Author Amy
40. Mr. Shields
42. For An-mei to say her mother's name was to spit on her father's ___
43. It is under the table leg in the kitchen.
44. The beads of An-mei's necklace from Second Wife were made of this
46. Directions

CROSSWORD ANSWER KEY - *The Joy Luck Club*

FILL IN THE BLANK QUIZ/WORKSHEET - *The Joy Luck Club*

Fill in the blank with the term that is described.

_____ 1. Waiting Between the _____

_____ 2. It burned An-mei the night her mother returned

_____ 3. Sleep; visit Mr. ___

_____ 4. Lena's profession

_____ 5. ___ Lady

_____ 6. Two ___

_____ 7. It ate the tears

_____ 8. Color of the candle

_____ 9. Ying-ying ___; Lena's mother

_____ 10. 'Pleading ___' Jing-mei's piano piece

_____ 11. This society gave Waverly her 2nd chess set

_____ 12. Waverly's game

_____ 13. Ying-ying fell off the __ and got separated from her family

_____ 14. The Twenty-six Malignant _____

_____ 15. ___ Face

_____ 16. He tormented Lena

_____ 17. For An-mei to say her mother's name was to spit on her father's ___

_____ 18. Rose's mother threw her blue sapphire one into the water

_____ 19. Substance First Wife used

_____ 20. Jing-mei's American name

_____ 21. Waverly's daughter

_____ 22. Where An-mei's family lived in China

_____ 23. Moon Lady became one

_____ 24. Lena's husband

146

MATCHING QUIZ/WORKSHEET - *Joy Luck Club*

___ 1. CHANG   A. Waiting Between the _____

___ 2. SHOSHANA   B. Rose's sister

___ 3. FAITH   C. Husband

___ 4. TAITAI   D. Proof of the rotting marriage

___ 5. MOLE   E. Jing-mei goes there to find her sisters

___ 6. CHINA   F. Lena's profession

___ 7. FOUR   G. Ying-ying ____; Lena's mother

___ 8. ARCHITECT   H. Huang ___: Tyan-yu's mother

___ 9. JUNE   I. On the third day after her mother died, An-mei learned to do this

___ 10. DOUBLE   J. He tormented Lena

___ 11. STCLAIR   K. It ate the tears

___ 12. ARNOLD   L. Waverly's daughter

___ 13. COOKIE   M. ___ Luck Club

___ 14. JANICE   N. ____ Lady

___ 15. SHANGHEI   O. Lindo Jong's daughter

___ 16. RICE   P. ____ Directions

___ 17. MOON   Q. Jing-mei's American name

___ 18. TREES   R. Ying-ying's daughter

___ 19. JOY   S. Waverly wants to go there for her second honeymoon

___ 20. BRIGHTNESS   T. An-mei and Lindo met at the ___ factory

___ 21. WAVERLY   U. Necklace made of red jade

___ 22. LENA   V. Festival of Pure ___

W. Rose defines it as an illusion that one is somehow in control

X. Face

ANSWER KEYS FILL IN THE BLANK AND MATCHING - *Joy Luck Club*

Fill in the Blank	Matching
1. TREES	1. U
2. SOUP	2. L
3. CHOU	3. W
4. ARCHITECT	4. H
5. MOON	5. D
6. KINDS	6. S
7. TURTLE	7. P
8. RED	8. F
9. ST. CLAIR	9. Q
10. CHILD	10. X
11. TAO	11. G
12. CHESS	12. J
13. BOAT	13. T
14. GATES	14. B
15. DOUBLE	15. E
16. ARNOLD	16. C
17. GRAVE	17. N
18. RING	18. A
19. OPIUM	19. M
20. JUNE	20. V
21. SHOSHANA	21. O
22. NINGPO	22. R
23. MAN	
24. ARNOLD	

JUGGLE LETTER REVIEW GAME CLUE SHEET - *The Joy Luck Club*

YOJ	JOY	___ Luck Club
NUEJ	JUNE	Jing-mei's American name
LIWENIK	KWEILIN	Original setting for JLC meetings
CUYLK	LUCKY	The women hoped to be __ and that was their only joy.
CAJEIN	JANICE	Rose's sister
HASEINGH	SHANGHEI	Jing-mei goes there to find her sisters
OOPP	POPO	An-mei's name for her grandmother
GOINPN	NINGPO	Where An-mei's family lived in China
VAREG	GRAVE	For An-mei to say her mother's name was to spit on her father's ___
HOUS	SHOU	Having no respect for ancestors or family
OPUS	SOUP	It burned An-mei the night her mother returned
DER	RED	Color of the candle
YELVAWR	WAVERLY	Lindo Jong's daughter
NYATUY	TYANYU	Lindo's husband via the matchmaker
ITAAIT	TAITAI	Huang ___: Tyan-yu's mother
VELTERSOF	LEFTOVERS	Meaning of 'yu' in Tyan-yu's name
NYATUIA	TAIYUAN	Lindo's village
NEEVAH	HEAVEN	Jong family hill: Three Steps to ___
GHANC	CHANG	Necklace made of red jade
CLADEN	CANDLE	It was supposed to be lit at both ends and kept burning all night.
YEWERLJ	JEWELRY	Matchmaker suggested Lindo take off all her to be better balanced
LOME	MOLE	Proof of the rotting marriage
THINSGERSB	BRIGHTNESS	Festival of Pure ___
ONOM	MOON	___ Lady
DOLBO	BLOOD	Ying-ying got it on her clothes
OBAT	BOAT	Ying-ying fell off the __ and got separated from her family
ANM	MAN	Moon Lady became one
NSU	SUN	Moon Lady's husband lives there
DUFON	FOUND	Ying-ying's wish was to be ___
SLURE	RULES	___ of the Game
TAR	ART	Lindo taught Waverly the ___ of invisible strength
IEMMIE	MEIMEI	Waverly's family called her this

SHECS	CHESS	Waverly's game
TINNEVC	VINCENT	He actually got the chess set for Christmas
VEESLARSIF	LIFESAVERS	They took the place of the white knight and black pawn
OPALU	LAUPO	Waverly's neighbor who played chess with her
OAT	TAO	This society gave Waverly her 2nd chess set
GRETI	TIGER	Lena's mother's Chinese sign
IVOEC	VOICE	___ From the Wall
LIBBE	BIBLE	It is under the table leg in the kitchen.
DET	TED	Rose's husband
HITFA	FAITH	Rose defines it as an illusion that one is somehow in control.
STAGE	GATES	*The Twenty-six Malignant* _____
GNIB	BING	He drowned
NIRG	RING	Rose's mother threw her blue sapphire one into the water
DSINK	KINDS	Two ____
NOIPA	PIANO	Instrument Jing-mei played
ZAMIGENAS	MAGAZINES	Jing-mei's mother looked at these for stories about exceptional children
GHNUC	CHUNG	Piano teacher
DHICL	CHILD	"Pleading ___" Jing-mei's piano piece
CEIR	RICE	_____ Husband
LODC	COLD	If the lips are gone, the teeth will be ___.
DLAROH	HAROLD	Lena's husband
DLANRO	ARNOLD	He tormented Lena
ORFU	FOUR	_____ Directions
NASSOHAH	SHOSHANA	Waverly's daughter
CHIR	RICH	Mr. Shields
OWOD	WOOD	Without ____
UCOH	CHOU	Sleep; visit Mr. ___
NAT	TAN	Author Amy
ILQYATU	QUALITY	Best ____
BARC	CRAB	One with a lost leg on Chinese New Year is a bad sign
RULETT	TURTLE	It ate the tears
SIGAMEP	MAGPIES	The eggs from the turtle's beak produced seven of these
SWUTGIN	WUTSING	He owned house where An-mei and her mother lived
NAY	YAN	An-mei's personal maid; __ Chang
SLAGS	GLASS	The beads of An-mei's necklace from Second Wife were made of this

OMUPI	OPIUM	Substance First Wife used
THOUS	SHOUT	On the third day after her mother died, An-mei learned to do this
STREE	TREES	Waiting Between the _____
NALE	LENA	Ying-ying's daughter
TACRECTHI	ARCHITECT	Lena's profession
HIWUS	WUSHI	Where Ying-ying grew up
LOUDEB	DOUBLE	___ Face
NICAH	CHINA	Waverly wants to go there for her second honeymoon
KOEIOC	COOKIE	An-mei and Lindo met at the ___ factory
SCITTEK	TICKETS	A Pair of ___
NAUUSY	SUYUAN	Jing-mei's mother; ___ Woo
SUH	HSU	An-mei ___; Rose ___ Jordan
NODIL	LINDO	Waverly's mother
SLITRAC	ST. CLAIR	Ying-ying ____; Lena's mother

VOCABULARY RESOURCE MATERIALS

VOCABULARY WORD SEARCH - *The Joy Luck Club*

All the words in this list are associated with **The Joy Luck Club** with emphasis on the vocabulary words being studied in the unit. The words are placed backwards, forward, diagonally, up and down. The clues below the word search will help identify the words used.

```
S U O I V E D E T C A R T X E T A V I T L U C R
T H T S N S E H C G B R T B X N V T J D V N H W
U T A M M V T S I L A O H L T T G O M B E C A W
N C U B Y I A W V P N T E O R C J U M C H A S M
N T T M B D R D E R D C O A A K T T L L E N T N
E C N V A Y T K E O O A L T V E C E R F M N I B
D X A C K C E S G D N F O E A D Q D U E E Y S H
G I I N I Z N A A I E E G D G P H X S S N D E Y
N C N N O E E C R G D N Y E A K O R E R C O R F
I T O S T P P R O Y I E B R N Q P S N O E W E K
V R D E O G Y I F H M B T E T U R G T M X R V D
I W R C J L W D T O R D L P Z P I S I E B Y E Y
V P A W T V E A K E Y A C A Z A S N N R R T R Z
E M B F B T O N B J G E N T Q R T X E D P I M Q
R D E D U L E M T E X C R J V D I V L U Y Z T F
M D E N A W O E R O C N E D I O N A R A P X W Y
E S U O P S U R V E Y E D N H N E E P O R T E R
```

ABANDONED	DRAB	INVADED	REGAL	TAPERED
ACRID	ELUDED	IRONIC	REMORSE	TAUT
BENEFACTOR	ENCORE	LOATHING	REVERE	THEOLOGY
BLOATED	ENGULFED	MUTE	REVIVING	TOUTED
CANOPY	ERUPTED	PARANOID	RUSE	UNCANNY
CHASM	EVICT	PARDON	SENTINEL	VAIN
CHASTISE	EXTRACTED	PENETRATE	SHABBY	VEHEMENCE
CICADAS	EXTRAVAGANT	PORTER	SMIRK	WANED
CULTIVATE	FORAGE	POSTERITY	SOMBER	
DEFTLY	FOYER	PRETENSE	SPOUSE	
DEVIOUS	GENUINE	PRISTINE	STUNNED	
DOWRY	INSOLENT	PRODIGY	SURVEYED	

VOCABULARY CROSSWORD - *Joy Luck Club*

VOCABULARY CROSSWORD CLUES - *The Joy Luck Club*

ACROSS
1. Allowing some light to pass through
6. To put out, throw out or expel
8. Serious
10. Left-overs
12. Insects that make high-pitched, droning sound
14. Of substandard quality
15. Contrary to what is expected
17. Pulled out
20. Plotting to achieve an evil or illegal end
22. A crafty strategy or plan
25. Tight
27. Speechless
30. Entrance hall
31. Having an extreme fear or distrust of others
34. Conceited; proud
35. Escaped the understanding of
37. Royal
38. Entered by force to conquer
39. Treat with respect
40. Divert

DOWN
1. Clear
2. Unpleasant to the taste or smell
3. Cooking just below the boiling point
4. Completely in agreement
5. Word for word
7. Abyss; gorge; steep-sided hole
9. Small or deficient in quantity
11. Guard
13. Grow; encourage; promote
14. Scampered
16. Decreased
18. Money or property brought by a bride to her husband
19. Arrogant; presumptuous and insulting
21. Real
23. Plan
24. Offensively self-satisfied
26. Deserted; left
28. Publicly praised
29. Future generations
30 To make a thorough search for
32. Skillfully
33. Cherished; having value; beloved
36. Dull

VOCABULARY CROSSWORD ANSWER KEY - *Joy Luck Club*

VOCABULARY WORKSHEET 1 - *The Joy Luck Club*

____ 1. MEAGER   A. very loud, deep sounds

____ 2. PODIATRIST   B. having an extreme fear or distrust of others

____ 3. PRESUMPTUOUS   C. guard

____ 4. REMORSE   D. to put out, throw out or expel

____ 5. TOUTED   E. contrary to what is expected

____ 6. REMNANTS   F. publicly praised

____ 7. CICADAS   G. real

____ 8. RADICALLY   H. entrance hall

____ 9. INVADED   I. plan

____ 10. BELLOWS   J. foot doctor

____ 11. TRANSLUCENT   K. astounded; dazed

____ 12. STRATEGY   L. entered by force to conquer

____ 13. ENGULFED   M. bringing back to life

____ 14. EVICT   N. insects that make high-pitched, droning sound

____ 15. MUTE   O. small or deficient in quantity

____ 16. STUNNED   P. excessively forward

____ 17. IRONIC   Q. feeling of regret for one's misdeeds or sins

____ 18. SCHEMING   R. allowing some light to pass through

____ 19. REVIVING   S. plotting to achieve an evil or illegal end

____ 20. PARANOID   T. left-overs

____ 21. GENUINE   U. pierce; force into

____ 22. SENTINEL   V. speechless

____ 23. PENETRATE   W. departing from the norm; extremely

____ 24. FOYER   X. surrounded by something almost to the point of being lost in it

____ 25. DRAB   Y. dull

VOCABULARY WORKSHEET 2 - *The Joy Luck Club*

___ 1. abyss; gorge; steep-sided hole
    a. sentinel   b. chasm   c. forage   d. pretense

___ 2. introductory occurrence or statement
    a. inventory   b. sauciness   c. preamble   d. simmering

___ 3. of little importance
    a. trivial   b. extracted   c. pardon   d. cunning

___ 4. tight
    a. penetrate   b. verbatim   c. taut   d. canopy

___ 5. completely in agreement
    a. bellows   b. trivial   c. unanimously   d. stunned

___ 6. in perfect condition
    a. cautiously   b. pristine   c. precious   d. prospect

___ 7. pierce; force into
    a. simmering   b. benefactor   c. penetrate   d. cautiously

___ 8. forgive
    a. revere   b. stagnant   c. pardon   d. vulnerable

___ 9. swelled up
    a. taut   b. bloated   c. vehemence   d. trivial

___ 10. astounded; dazed
    a. foyer   b. remorse   c. inventory   d. stunned

___ 11. plan
    a. strategy   b. reviving   c. somber   d. covenant

___ 12. deserted; left
    a. inventory   b. trivial   c. abandoned   d. foyer

___ 13. motionless
    a. shabby   b. inevitable   c. stagnant   d. vehemence

___ 14. statement
    a. declaration   b. remnants   c. trivial   d. deftly

___ 15. roof-like covering
    a. canopy   b. uncanny   c. irrational   d. stagnant

___ 16. at the end of patience; irritated
    a. abandoned   b. exasperated   c. spouse   d. waned

___ 17. publicly praised
    a. engulfed   b. sauciness   c. touted   d. mute

___ 18. deserving strong dislike; vile
    a. despicable   b. mute   c. bloated   d. sauciness

___ 19. taking a count of
    a. laments   b. insolent   c. inventory   d. cunning

___ 20. cherished; having value; beloved
    a. precious   b. inventory   c. canopy   d. inevitable

KEY: VOCABULARY WORKSHEETS - *The Joy Luck Club*

Worksheet 1	Worksheet 2
1. O	1. B
2. J	2. C
3. P	3. A
4. Q	4. C
5. F	5. C
6. T	6. B
7. N	7. C
8. W	8. C
9. L	9. B
10. A	10. D
11. R	11. A
12. I	12. C
13. X	13. C
14. D	14. A
15. V	15. A
16. K	16. B
17. E	17. C
18. S	18. A
19. M	19. C
20. B	20. A
21. G	
22. C	
23. U	
24. H	
25. Y	

VOCABULARY JUGGLE LETTER REVIEW GAME CLUES - *The Joy Luck Club*

SCRAMBLED	WORD	CLUE
BAHBYS	SHABBY	of substandard quality
RUCERDIS	SCURRIED	scampered
GEMREA	MEAGER	small or deficient in quantity
MESRBO	SOMBER	serious
LOSNUMYNAIU	UNANIMOUSLY	completely in agreement
ANRULETSCNT	TRANSLUCENT	allowing some light to pass through
TATLVIECU	CULTIVATE	grow; encourage; promote
ERUPICSO	PRECIOUS	cherished; having value; beloved
YOUVOGLIRS	VIGOROUSLY	done with force or energy
WROYD	DOWRY	money or property brought by a bride to her husband
NONSITEL	INSOLENT	arrogant; presumptuous and insulting
DOEATLB	BLOATED	swelled up
TEMU	MUTE	speechless
NEGEIUN	GENUINE	real
DACCSAI	CICADAS	insects that make high-pitched, droning sound
TPTEENARE	PENETRATE	pierce; force into
SPETEERN	PRETENSE	false appearance
IDDNAVE	INVADED	entered by force to conquer
RLCAOIEDNAT	DECLARATION	statement
SOLUFRREEM	REMORSEFUL	regretful; sorrowful
TTXADRCEE	EXTRACTED	pulled out
GMMRISNIE	SIMMERING	cooking just below the boiling point
DARIC	ACRID	unpleasant to the taste or smell
RYPSTEITO	POSTERITY	future generations
RARTSANNTEP	TRANSPARENT	clear
DAWNE	WANED	decreased
DEERPUT	ERUPTED	became violently active; exploded
SULNOILI	ILLUSION	false perception of reality
RAYSTTEG	STRATEGY	plan
DEELUD	ELUDED	escaped the understanding of
LDYTEF	DEFTLY	skillfully
RIDCATTS	DISTRACT	divert
UOETTD	TOUTED	publicly praised
HAMCS	CHASM	abyss; gorge; steep-sided hole
ARPNDO	PARDON	forgive
YLSIUUTACO	CAUTIOUSLY	carefully
NTSGAATN	STAGNANT	motionless

www.ingramcontent.com/pod-product-compliance
Lightning Source LLC
Chambersburg PA
CBHW051409070526
44584CB00023B/3354